SHAWN DAWSON

THE FORAGER'S DINNER

Finding, harvesting, and preparing Newfoundland and Labrador's edible plants

BOULDER
BOOKS

Library and Archives Canada Cataloguing in Publication

Title: The forager's dinner : finding, harvesting, and preparing Newfoundland and Labrador's edible plants / Shawn Dawson.
Names: Dawson, Shawn, 1988- author.
Description: Includes index.
Identifiers: Canadiana 20200321544 | ISBN 9781989417263 (softcover)
Subjects: LCSH: Wild plants, Edible—Newfoundland and Labrador—Identification. | LCSH: Cooking (Wild foods) | LCGFT: Cookbooks.
Classification: LCC QK98.5.C3 D38 2020 | DDC 581.6/3209718—dc23

© 2020 Shawn Dawson
Published by Boulder Books
Portugal Cove-St. Philip's, Newfoundland and Labrador
www.boulderbooks.ca

Design and layout: Tanya Montini
Cover photo: Ritche Perez
Editor: Stephanie Porter
Copy editor: Iona Bulgin

Printed in Canada

Excerpts from this publication may be reproduced under licence from Access Copyright, or with the express written permission of Boulder Books Ltd., or as permitted by law. All rights are otherwise reserved and no part of this publications may be reproduced, stored in a retrieval system, or transmitted in any form or by any means, electronic, mechanical, photocopying, scanning, recording, or otherwise, except as specifically authorized.

We acknowledge the financial support of the Government of Newfoundland and Labrador through the Department of Tourism, Culture, Industry and Innovation.

THE FORAGER'S DINNER

In memory of my grandmother
Lorraine Kavanagh.

Thank you for teaching me that dandelions
are more than weeds.

TABLE OF CONTENTS

FOREWORD by *Celeste Mah* 13

INTRODUCTION 15

HOW TO USE THIS BOOK 17

SPRING SHOOTS 25
Clover 26
Corn Lily 28
Dandelion 30
    Pasta with Dandelion Pesto and Mussels *Sylvie Mitford,
The Boreal Diner* 34
Fiddlehead 36
Fireweed 38
    Fireweed Jelly *Maria Martin* 40
Goutweed 42
Japanese Knotweed 44
    Knotweed Jam *Nick Van Mele, The Grounds Café* 49
Stinging Nettle 50
    Nettle Pesto *Shawn Dawson* 53
    Cream of Nettle Soup *Sylvie Mitford, The Boreal Diner* 54
Wintercress 56
Yarrow 58

EAT YOUR WEEDS 61
Chickweed 62
Lamb's Quarter 64
    Lamb's Quarter and Brown Quinoa Porridge
Kyle Puddester, Fork 66
Pennycress 68

Pineappleweed 70
    Toasted Milk Pineappleweed Cream and Strawberries
    Celeste Mah, Raymonds 72
Plantain 74
Shepherd's Purse 76
Sorrel and Curly Dock 78
    Sorrel and Mushroom Risotto *Chris Mercer, Brewdock* 82
Stonecrop 84
Roast Lamb with Stonecrop, Caramelized Honey,
    and Tzatziki *Matthew Swift, Terre Restaurant* 86

BEACH GREENS 89

Beach Pea 90
Goosetongue 92
Orach 94
Oysterleaf 96
Roseroot 98
Sandwort 100
    Beach Green Coleslaw *Shawn Dawson* 103
Scotch Lovage 104
    Shawn's Love Butter *Shawn Dawson* 107
Sea Rocket 108
Strand Wheat 110

FRESHWATER WEEDS 113

Cattails 114
    Cattail Blini *Ross Larkin, Raymonds* 116
River Mint 118
    Moose Shank with Mint + Lovage *Lori McCarthy, Cod Sounds* 120
Watercress 122
Wild Basil 124

SEAWEEDS ... 127
Bladderwrack ... 128
Oarweed ... 130
    Sea Olives *Shawn Dawson* ... 132
Red Dulse ... 134
Sea Lettuce ... 136
Sugar Kelp ... 138
    Seaweed Salad *Courtney + Terrence Howell, Grates Cove Studios* ... 140

EAT THE TREES (AND SHRUBS) ... 143
Alder ... 144
Balsam Fir ... 148
Birch ... 150
Juniper ... 152
    Juniper Smoked Lamb *Colin Moïse, Renegade Harvest* ... 154
Labrador Tea ... 156
Maple ... 158
Spruce ... 162
    Spruce Tip Mortadella *Shaun Hussey, Chinched* ... 166
Sweet Gale ... 168
Tamarack ... 170

FORGOTTEN FRUITS AND GARDENS ... 173
Apple ... 174
    Rosehip and Crabapple Jam *Elke Dettmer, Points East Guesthouse* ... 177
Black Elderberry ... 178
Currants ... 180
Damson ... 182
    Damson Plum Chutney *Karen Willoughby, Handmade by Hand* ... 185
Forsythia ... 186
Lilac ... 188
    Lilac + Honey Pie *Stephanie Mackenzie, Woodstock Public House* ... 190
Plum ... 192
Rhubarb ... 194
    Rhubarb-Crow-Chuckley Chutney *Amy Anthony* ... 196
Wild Hops ... 198

BERRIES 203

Bakeapple 204
    Warm Bakeapple Scrunchion Vinaigrette with Lemon Pepper Cod and Vegetable Succotash *Mark McCrowe* 206

Blackberry 210

Blueberry 212

Bunchberry 214

Chokeberry 216

Chokecherry 218

Chuckley Pear 220

Cranberry 222

Creeping Snowberry 224

Crowberry 226

Dewberry 228

Dogberry 230

High-bush Cranberry 232

Northern Wild Raisin 234

Partridgeberry 236
    Partridgeberry Cake *Kayla O'Brien, Fork* 238

Pin Cherry 240

Raspberry 242
    Campfire-Cooked Raspberry Upside-down Cake *Kevin Massey, The Old Dublin Bakery* 244

Rose 246
    Rose + Rhubarb Cocktail *Jessica Gibson, Toslow* 248

Skunk Currant 250
    Skunk Currant Pie *Nick Giles* 252

Squashberry 254

Wild Haskap 256

Wild Strawberry 258
    Wild Strawberry Jam-Jams *Graham + Kelly Parisien, Nourish* 260

FLOWER POWER 263

Blue Marsh Violet 265
Coltsfoot 265
Forget-Me-Not 265
Marsh Marigold 265
Oxeye Daisy 267
Queen Ann's Lace 267

LICHEN IT 269

Caribou Moss 270
    Caribou Moss Two Ways *Nick King, Ollie's Pasta* 272

Index by common name 275
Index by scientific name 276
Photo credits 277
Acknowledgements 278
About Shawn Dawson 280

FOREWORD

Flossman Dandy Cabbage? What? Who is this guy? You mean he just shows up with things he has found in the woods? What kind of things, exactly?

That's what went through my head five and a half years ago when I moved to Newfoundland and started working at Raymonds as their pastry chef. I was obviously intrigued and couldn't wait to meet this guy I was hearing so much about.

Finally, one day, Shawn Dawson showed up with all of these beautiful wild edibles I didn't know much about—pineappleweed, creeping snowberries, and dolgo apples. My understanding of the bounty of local ingredients available in my new home expanded beyond my wildest dreams. Dawson and I pretty much had our very own meet-cute that day. You know, like that moment in a romantic comedy where the future couple meets for the first time? Except in real life, I was already engaged and our meet-cute was one sparked purely by a mutual respect for each other's craft, and one that quickly grew into a great friendship.

Dawson's love for Newfoundland and everything the land has to offer has definitely had an impact not only on my desserts but on my life as well. I can no longer walk by weeds on the street or on hikes without acknowledging the edible delicacies underfoot: "Oh! Pineappleweed! I should pick some and make ice cream!" Or, "Ahhh, look at all those berries! What are they? I should send a photo to Dawson!"

Our friendship has also led to collaboration. One day we had a conversation about chanterelle ice cream. I was a bit skeptical at first but Dawson was convinced I could turn it into something delicious.

We made a deal: he would dehydrate a bunch of smaller chanterelles and bring them to me for free, and in turn I would make ice cream for the both of us to try. Guess what? It was one of the best damn ice creams I've ever made and chanterelles have seen their way onto my dessert menu in many different forms since.

My instincts about Dawson have proven true ever since our meet-cute that day: his passion and enthusiasm for the province's edible riches are unparalleled. There is so much to this land that most of us know little about—local knowledge and experience that Dawson holds. I'm so glad he's willing to let us all in on his little secrets with this book, and I know it will inspire a new generation of people interested in exploring forests, fields, and shorelines for delicious treats.

Celeste Mah
Pastry Chef, Raymonds Restaurant, St. John's
Canada's Best Pastry Chef 2019 (Canada's 100 Best)

TAKE A HIKE ON THE WILD SIDE

Japanese knotweed is a superfood. There. I said it.

Before farming, there was foraging. Instead of selectively growing crops and relying on international shipping networks for a wide range of choice and options all year long, we ate whatever was in season. That led to a greater appreciation for natural growing cycles, for learning to gather food at its peak and preserving it for later.

Today, harvesting wild food is driven by a renewed interest in the plants that grow around us. Issues of food security are at play, but so is a desire to eat a greater diversity of plants. To try new flavours and to think differently about the plants we overlook or forcefully remove. How much time do gardeners spend removing dandelions? They are some of the healthiest foods you can put in your body.

Harvesting and learning to prepare wild food makes you a better cook. If you stumble across a patch of blackberries, river mint, or Scotch lovage, seize the opportunity to try something new.

General harvesting guidelines

When harvesting edible plants from the wild, ask yourself a few simple questions:

1. **Am I harvesting from a safe environment?**
   If you are harvesting river mint from a ditch with stagnant, unmoving water, for example, the answer to this question is no. Be sure you are not in a heavily polluted area, beside a busy road, or near any outfalls; avoid gardens, lawns, or other areas that may have been sprayed with pesticides.

   Make sure you're not in a protected area. If you wish to forage on private property, secure permission first.

2. **Am I harvesting sustainably?**
   We are lucky to live in a place with extensive untouched land full of mother nature's bounty. Food is around us, everywhere you look! There's enough food here on the island that if we harvest sustainably we can feed our families and preserve enough to last us through the winter.

   Always leave some food and plants behind. A rule of thumb: leave at least 25 to 30 per cent of what you are picking—you want to leave enough berries for the wildlife to eat (and poop out in other locations), enough flowers for the bees to pollinate, enough seeds to propagate. Always leave enough new growth on trees so they will flourish and provide more for us each year.

   If you arrive in an area that has evidently already been harvested, move on and find a fresh patch. Never take more than you need.

   Do not use ATVs in bogs and marshes to harvest berries; they damage our wetlands.

   Never use a berry rake to pick berries. This weakens the berry bushes, stripping most of the leaves and damaging the wood. Not to mention you're making more work cleaning the berries when you get home.

3. **Are the plants I'm harvesting safe to eat? Does the plant have any dangerous look-alikes?**
   Before you harvest, make sure you know what plant you are dealing with. Get familiar with the edible plants in your area. Take lots of photographs and do your homework before you cook or consume a wild edible. Search reputable sources online, consult field guides (including this book), and talk to others with experience. Take a foraging tour or ask to accompany a seasoned picker in your area.

   Plants in the carrot family should be harvested with caution; there are a number of toxic plants in this family.

HOW TO USE THIS BOOK

This book is divided into several categories, by use or location/habitat. A number of species could easily fall into more than one category (blueberry bushes are a shrub, for example, but you'll find the description under "berries," for which the plant is best known). If you are looking for a specific species, check the table of contents or the index.

Throughout the pages, you'll find recipes contributed by many of the province's top chefs, showcasing their use of foraged foods. It is my hope that these recipes will inspire you to try new recipes and techniques—and check out some of the exciting restaurants in the province.

Sections

Spring shoots: The first edible plants to emerge after a long, cold winter. Includes tender early shoots and greens.

Eat your weeds: From late spring through the summer, look in your own backyard for these species. Hated by gardeners, beloved by foragers.

Beach greens: Along the rocky and sandy coastal beaches of Newfoundland, where the tide meets the shore.

Freshwater weeds: Check the banks of rivers, ponds, and streams around the island for these finds.

Seaweeds: Superfoods from the North Atlantic Ocean.

Eat the trees (+ shrubs): From Labrador tea to spruce tips, don't forget to eat your trees.

Forgotten fruits + gardens: Fruit trees, vines, and other homestead escapes that have survived the test of time.

Berries: Over 20 species of wild fruits and berries found across Newfoundland.

Flower power: Buds and blossoms to brighten any salad or other wild food dish.

Lichen it: Neither plant nor fungus, but worth a taste.

SAMPLE PAGE

Common name —

Other common names if applicable —

Latin name —

Icons for the edible/preferred parts of the plant are dark. See legend. —

Basic description for identification purposes, including where the species may be found —

Notes on when and how to harvest, which parts of the plant to take, and specific considerations for sustainable foraging —

Basic information on popular uses for the plants. Includes relevant warnings and cautions —

EAT YOUR WEEDS

LAMB'S QUARTER

Goosefoot, wild spinach, wild quinoa
Chenopodium album L.

WHAT IS IT?

Lamb's quarter spreads quickly in a variety of habitats, i beaches, compost piles, roadsides, and other disturbed usually 30 to 50 centimetres tall but can reach 1 metre leaves are an elongated diamond shape. Younger leaves a sugar-coated. Clustered greenish flowers develop a red h produce round seeds.

Frequently called wild spinach or goosefoot (for the sh Lamb's quarter is actually related to quinoa (*Chenopodiu*

HOW TO HARVEST

Collect young shoots or leaves in the spring; look for centimetres long or less for the best salad greens. Pick t all season long.

Harvest flowers in the fall, when they turn reddish.

HOW TO USE

Leaves have a pleasant nutty, spinach-like taste and are a wild green salad. Greens harvested later in the summer a cooked dishes than salads. Steam, add to stir-fries or so store for winter use.

Treat the flower as you would quinoa: boil in water u and serve as porridge or a side dish, or toast in the oven.

Lamb's quarter leaves contain some oxalic acid and sh in moderation. Cooking removes this acid. Seeds contai may be mildly toxic and should not be consumed in exces

Indicates the months the species can *most often* be harvested. This is approximate and varies by region and by year

Habitats in which you are most likely to see the species appear in colour. See habitat descriptions next page

EAT YOUR WEEDS

THE FORAGER'S DINNER

Icons

Flower, leaves/needles, root, shoots, stem, seed, fruit

An X indicates a plant part is toxic and should not be eaten.

Habitat descriptions

Banks and shores: Gravel and sandy beaches, as well as riverbanks and other fresh- and saltwater shorelines.

Barrens: Exposed rocky outcrops, scrubby plateaus, windswept headlands, and hills. Although barrens may appear bleak and the plant life short in stature, they are home to a diversity of species.

Clearings: Meadows, fields, and other open areas scattered throughout the forest.

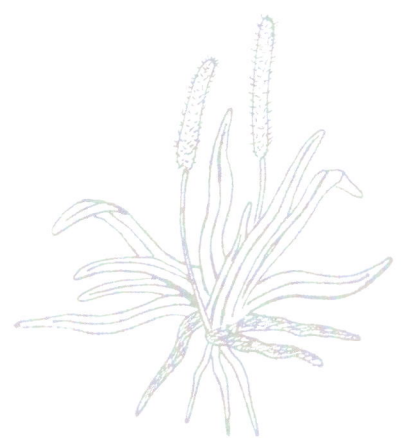

Disturbed areas: Gardens, lawns, roadsides, parking lots, gravel pits, and other areas that have been cleared of their original vegetation, usually near or in communities.

Forest: Many of the trees making up the boreal forest of Newfoundland are edible; other edible species thrive on the forest floor.

Wetlands: Bogs, fens, and marshes are home to herbs, shrubs, lichens, and dwarfed trees.

SPRING SHOOTS

Perhaps the most exciting part of the foraging year is when the early tender shoots emerge after a long Newfoundland winter. When maple sap starts flowing, spring is just around the corner. The welcome sights of purple nettle tips, dandelion greens, and the pink crowns of Japanese knotweed aren't far behind.

Getting out after the snow melts to harvest for fresh salads, teas, pesto, and preserves is a time to anticipate. Collecting, cooking, and eating nutrient-dense spring shoots rejuvenate the body and mind.

This section features some of the first edible species you'll find in the spring. Most of these "weeds" are invasive species, found in disturbed areas in and near communities. In other words, you won't have to travel far to pick the first salad of the season.

SPRING SHOOTS

SPRING SHOOTS

CLOVER

White, red, and alsike clover
Trifolium repens, T. pretense, T. hybridum

May - September

WHAT IS IT?

Clover, a widespread cosmopolitan flowering plant, is most often found in gardens, fields, and lawns. Its green leaves have three leaflets (four, if you're lucky); spiky flower heads are a favourite of bees and other pollinators. Alsike clover flowers are pink and white; red clover is purple-red. These two species have upright stems and can grow to 30 to 40 centimetres tall. White clover grows to about 10 to 15 centimetres, and its white flowers are smaller than those of the other two species.

Clover flower heads each contain 20 to 50 tubular flowers. Pluck out individual flowers and suck on the ends to extract the nectar and enjoy the honey-like flavour.

HOW TO HARVEST

Pick plants and leaves when they emerge, and flower heads when they are in bloom.

HOW TO USE

Shoots and young leaves are tender salad greens. Add flowers to salads or use as a garnish. Steep fresh or dried flower heads for tea.

SPRING SHOOTS

SPRING SHOOTS

CORN LILY

Clintonia borealis

May - June

WHAT IS IT?

Corn lily grows in mats on the forest floor and other shaded areas, often in stands of spruce and fir trees—the same places you'll find bunchberries. Plants have two to four large (up to 20 centimetres long) oval leaves. A single stalk grows from the centre of the rosette of leaves.

Greenish flowers at the stalk tips are followed by round, shiny blue berries. Corn lily berries are toxic.

HOW TO HARVEST

Cut leaves at their base in late spring when they are still dark green and before flowers emerge.

HOW TO USE

Corn lily leaves have a bright, fresh, cucumber-like flavour. Sauté for a side dish or use fresh in salads. Try a salad of corn lily leaves with a vinaigrette of olive oil and apple cider vinegar and sprinkled with feta cheese.

Do not eat corn lily flowers or berries.

SPRING SHOOTS

SPRING SHOOTS

DANDELION

Taraxacum officinale

May - June

WHAT IS IT?

If you are just beginning to gather and consume wild food, dandelion is the ideal plant to start with. This easily identified, early spring harvest is bountiful and rich in nutrients, including potassium, calcium, iron, and vitamins A and C.

Dandelion is a herbaceous perennial. Its arrowhead-shaped leaves are long and narrow, up to 30 centimetres in length, with jagged toothed edges. Each plant has a single disc-shaped deep yellow flower 2 to 5 centimetres in diameter growing at the end of a hollow stalk. Flowers open during the day and close at night. Dandelion has a long taproot.

Dandelion is considered to be the plant of milk and honey: according to some, cows that eat dandelion have increased milk production; flowers are important sources of pollen and nectar for bees in the spring.

HOW TO HARVEST

Dandelion can be found virtually everywhere in Newfoundland—in disturbed areas, lawns, gardens, fields, and gravel lots.

Harvest leaves and buds before the plant flowers; after flowering, the leaves become bitter.

When harvesting dandelion roots, use a shovel; it can be almost impossible to pull up the entire root by hand. If you are trying to keep the dandelions at bay, try not to snap off the roots as you harvest. Small pieces of roots left in the ground will quickly develop into more plants.

SPRING SHOOTS

HOW TO USE

Every part of the dandelion, from bloom to root, is edible. Eat young leaves as you would spinach. Traditionally, in Newfoundland dandelion greens were served with Jiggs' dinner on Sundays. Gather young flower buds for pickles or capers, or serve as you would fresh peas. Use the flowers for tea, wine, and beer. Roast and grind dandelion roots as a coffee substitute.

SPRING SHOOTS

Pasta with Dandelion Pesto and Mussels

Sylvie Mitford, co-owner and head chef, The Boreal Diner, Bonavista

½ lb mussels per person
¼ cup dry white wine or vegetable stock for cooking the mussels
Dry spaghetti or linguine (100 g per person) or fresh pasta (200 g per person)
Salt for pasta water
Extra-virgin olive oil
½ cup cherry tomatoes per person
Lemon juice
1 tbsp butter per person

Pesto
2 cups (packed) freshly washed dandelion greens
6 cloves garlic
½ cup sunflower seeds
1 cup extra-virgin olive oil
½ cup freshly grated Parmesan

Make the pesto
Place all pesto ingredients in a food processor and purée until smooth, scraping down the sides of the bowl as needed to incorporate all the ingredients. If it is too thick, add more olive oil. This probably makes more pesto than you will need for this dish. Pack the unused portion into a jar and cover the surface with olive oil to prevent discolouring. It will keep in the refrigerator for a week; store in the freezer for longer.

Prepare mussels
Rinse and pick though the mussels and remove any that are open. Steam in a tightly lidded pot with the wine until they are all open,

Sylvie Mitford, left.

about 2 to 5 minutes. Allow to cool slightly, then pick the meat out of the shells, discarding any unopened shells. Set aside.

Prepare pasta
Bring a large pot of heavily salted water (salted like the ocean) to a boil. Cook the pasta until al dente.

Assemble the dish
While the pasta is cooking, heat the olive oil in a large sauté pan. Add the cherry tomatoes and cook on a medium-high heat until they blister and split slightly. Add the mussels and a heaping tablespoon of pesto per serving. Scoop the pasta directly from the water into the pan. Add 2 or 3 tablespoons of pasta cooking water per serving and stir to mix the pesto with the pasta. Raise the heat to high and add the butter. Cook, tossing or stirring vigorously until the sauce emulsifies, becomes glossy, and coats the surface of the pasta. Add more pasta cooking water if it appears greasy. Add salt and pepper to taste and a dash of lemon juice.

Serve immediately, topped with freshly grated Parmesan.

SPRING SHOOTS

FIDDLEHEAD

Ostrich fern
Matteuccia struthiopteris

April - June

WHAT IS IT?

Fiddleheads are unfurled fern fronds. Only one edible species exists in Newfoundland—the ostrich fern. All other ferns on the island are carcinogenic and should not be consumed. Ostrich fern, common on banks and other wet areas in western Newfoundland, are a rare spring treat on the Avalon Peninsula.

Ostrich ferns have a distinct U-shaped groove up the stem, similar to that in a celery stalk. This species can also be distinguished by its smooth, deep green skin; most other fern species have hairy or fuzzy skin. Several fiddleheads emerge from a single black crown.

HOW TO HARVEST

Pick fiddleheads when they are 10 to 15 centimetres tall, before the fronds have unfurled.

HOW TO USE

Blanch fiddleheads to ensure that they are fully cooked before eating.

Fry blanched fiddleheads with garlic and butter for a side dish; they can also be pickled, steamed, roasted, or fried.

Be sure to cook fiddleheads well; even the edible ostrich fern can cause stomach upset when undercooked.

SPRING SHOOTS

Banks & Shores

Barrens

Clearings

Disturbed Areas

Forest

Wetlands

SPRING SHOOTS

FIREWEED

Northern asparagus
Chamaenerion angustifolium

WHAT IS IT?

Fireweed is a perennial herbaceous flowering plant found across the island of Newfoundland in disturbed areas: along the edges of farmlands, sunny meadows, and roadsides and near the ocean. A pioneer species, fireweed earned its name because it is often the first plant to colonize an area after a forest fire. The young shoots, as well as leaves and flowers, are edible.

Fireweed grows 1.5 to 2 metres tall in large groups. It is recognized by its large spike of pink-purple flowers at the top of its stem. Its many leaves are narrow and wrinkled.

HOW TO HARVEST

Don't miss the short window for harvesting fireweed shoots—this plant grows quickly. Collect the young reddish shoots in late May to early June. Harvest until the leaves open up or until plants reach about 15 centimetres in height; after this point, the stems become fibrous and bitter.

Pluck shoots from the ground, being mindful to leave the majority of a patch to grow to flower; these plants are a favourite of honeybees. I have been harvesting from the same patches of fireweed for years and they continue to grow in abundance. Shoots wilt quickly; store upright in water to keep them fresh.

Harvest leaves throughout the season, though these become slightly bitter as the plant approaches flowering. Flower bud clusters and flowers can be harvested when they appear in mid- to late July.

SPRING SHOOTS

HOW TO USE

Use the young shoots like asparagus; they are delicious sautéed or roasted in butter. Shoots can be chopped and added to salads, or pickled.

Use leaves as you would spinach leaves. Eat fresh in salads or steam.

Add flowers to a salad or as a garnish. Use to make fireweed jelly or (fresh or dried) tea. Harvest flower bud clusters and cook as a vegetable.

Fireweed Jelly

Maria Martin

8 cups packed fireweed flowers, rinsed
4 cups water
4 cups white sugar or cane sugar
½ cup lemon juice (or less, to taste)
1 57-g package pectin

Boil 4 cups water. Let cool slightly, add the flowers, and steep for 20 minutes. Don't be alarmed if it turns a brownish colour.
    Strain the liquid through a cheesecloth. Discard the flowers.
    Bring the tea to a boil. Add the sugar, pectin, and lemon juice. The bright pink colour should magically come back!
    Bring back to a boil and simmer 15 minutes, stirring to ensure the sugar and pectin are dissolved.
    Test the jelly: place a couple of drops of jelly on a cold plate. Leave for a few minutes; if the jelly doesn't thicken, add more pectin or continue to simmer. Test every few minutes.
    Prepare jam jars. Ladle the jelly into the jars, seal, and process in a hot water bath for 10 minutes.
    Let cool for 24 hours. Store fireweed jelly in a cool, dark place to preserve the colour.

SPRING SHOOTS

SPRING SHOOTS

SPRING SHOOTS

GOUTWEED
Ground elder
Aegopodium podagraria

WHAT IS IT?
Goutweed, an invasive perennial, was brought to North America as an ornamental garden plant for ground cover. Found in many gardens, lawns, and other disturbed areas, goutweed is one of the more hated weeds in Newfoundland—it is often called "neighbour weed," because if your neighbour has it, you do too. Elsewhere in Canada, this plant is frequently called ground elder, as its leaves resemble those of elderberry trees.

Goutweed leaves are in groups of three toothed leaflets. Plants produce small clusters of tiny white flowers, but the primary method of propagation is via its long spaghetti-like rhizomes, which make it almost impossible to eradicate. Goutweed grows well in shaded, moist areas.

HOW TO HARVEST
Pick tender shoots in early spring—plants quickly become tough and fibrous.

HOW TO USE
Goutweed has a delicious peppery taste. Use the greens as you would spinach: steam or add to quiche, wild green pesto, or stir-fries.

SPRING SHOOTS

JAPANESE KNOTWEED

Fallopia japonica

May - June

WHAT IS IT?

Japaneese knotweed is without a doubt Newfoundland's most hated invasive species and every gardener's nightmare. Introduced to North America for erosion prevention and as an ornamental garden plant, it quickly spread. Despite its bad reputation (or because of it), Japanese knotweed is a perfect food to forage: delicious and nutritious, it grows in abundance and cannot be overharvested.

Japanese knotweed, a perennial of the knotweed and buckwheat family, is native to Japan and other parts of Asia. The shoots resemble those of asparagus and are olive green with traces of red with a bright pink crown and base.

Shoots mature to a hollow stem that grows to a height of 1 to 3 metres, with oval-shaped, olive to pale green leaves. Creamy white clusters of flowers grow about 10 centimetres long in late summer.

As kids, my friends and I used Japanese knotweed stalks to shoot dogberries at one another. I also have memories of chewing on them for their sour taste.

Japanese knotweed thrives in disturbed areas. It is shade-tolerant and also grows well in direct sunlight. Plants are commonly found on roadsides and in ditches, gardens, old homesteads, and along riverbeds. Once established, plants spread quickly due to its extensive root system. Knotweed can grow through pavement, concrete, and retaining walls.

If any piece of root is left in the ground, this plant can and will grow back.

SPRING SHOOTS

Banks & Shores
Barrens
Clearings
Disturbed Areas
Forest
Wetlands

SPRING SHOOTS

HOW TO HARVEST

Harvest new shoots early in the spring, as soon as you see the crowns emerging. There's a short window for harvesting; as Japanese knotweed really does seem to grow a "mile a minute." The smaller the shoots, the better the taste. Once they reach over 15 to 20 centimetres, they become more fibrous. Wearing gloves, bury your finger in the soil alongside the shoot and snap it off from the roots.

HOW TO USE

Treat Japanese knotweed shoots as you would asparagus—steam or sauté and serve with butter; they can also be pickled. Or treat them as you would rhubarb to make jam, jelly, or chutney.

SPRING SHOOTS

"A plant of a thousand names."
—Peter J. Scott

Japanese knotweed is known by many different names across the island of Newfoundland. An informal poll of the local Backyard Homesteaders Facebook page returned the following responses:

- Aunt-a-liens or acaleens (Burin Peninsula)
- Bamboo
- Bamboo balsam (St. Joseph's)
- Bean blowers (Bell Island)
- Blood trees
- Buckweed / buckwheat (southwest coast, Burgeo)
- Castor oil plant / castor oil tree (Southern Shore)
- Donkey rhubarb
- Mile-a-minute (Corner Brook, St. John's, Stephenville, etc.)
- Pea shooters
- Pipe tree
- Ramblers (Carbonear)
- Red legs
- Rhubarb bamboo (St. John's)
- Saraliens (Burin Peninsula)
- Scarlet runner (Burin Peninsula)
- September bloom
- September bride (west coast)
- September mist (Southern Shore; I grew up knowing this name)

SPRING SHOOTS

SPRING SHOOTS

Knotweed Jam

Nick Van Mele, head chef, The Grounds Café
Murray's Garden Centre, Portugal Cove-St. Philip's

2 lbs Japanese knotweed shoots, cleaned and diced
1 ½ cups sugar
½ cup water
1 lemon, juice and zest
1 red beet, peeled and grated (for colour)
Pinch of salt

Bring the knotweed, sugar, water, and salt to a boil. Add the lemon juice, zest, and grated beet.
    Simmer for 40 minutes. Cool and store in a Mason jar in the refrigerator.

Nick Van Mele.

SPRING SHOOTS

SPRING SHOOTS

STINGING NETTLE

Common nettle
Urtica dioica

WHAT IS IT?

Stinging nettle is a herbaceous perennial widespread across Newfoundland. Its leaves are lance- or heart-shaped, deeply toothed, hairy, and about twice as long as they are wide. Mature plants are 1 to 2 metres tall, or taller depending on soil conditions. The entire plant is covered in tiny, sharp hairs that irritate the skin when touched, giving the plant its common name. Bunches of tiny flowers may be white, green, or pinkish.

Stinging nettles are found in disturbed and nitrogen-rich soil. They are an invasive species in Newfoundland and often considered a nightmare by gardeners.

Stinging nettles are found around old barns, chicken coops, homesteads, gardens, and wharves and along roadsides and riverbeds.

HOW TO HARVEST

Stinging nettles can be harvested as soon as they emerge as spring shoots. Continue to harvest until the plants begin flowering, and become tough or covered in nettle caterpillars. It is much easier to harvest nettles without getting stung before they are large and mature.

Always wear gloves (preferably leather) and a long-sleeved shirt when harvesting to avoid the unpleasant stinging. You cannot overharvest this fast-growing and invasive species—in fact, I'm sure friends, family, or neighbours with nettles growing on their property will be more than happy to let you pick all that you want.

Harvest seeds in late August to September when they're green.

If you get stung when harvesting nettles, crush plantain or curled dock leaves and then apply to the burn to relieve some of the discomfort.

SPRING SHOOTS

HOW TO USE

Don't worry about stinging your mouth—the ability to sting goes away after the plants are boiled, steamed, or dried. Steam young leaves as a side dish or use in soups or stews. Boil or steam nettle leaves and then make pesto. Make tea from fresh or dried leaves.

Use seeds fresh or dried, as you would hemp seeds—add to cereal, yogurt, smoothies, or salads.

Nettle Pesto

Shawn Dawson

1 cup nettle tips, packed
2 tbsp (or more) toasted pine nuts, almonds, or sunflower seeds
Salt to taste
3 cloves garlic
3 tbsp grated Parmesan cheese
Olive oil

Rinse the nettles, being sure to remove any grass or dirt.

Blanch the nettles for 1 minute. Keep the water and drink as tea or use as food for your plants.

Remove the nettles from the boiling water and immediately plunge into an ice water bath to help keep the deep green colour.

Strain the nettles, turn out onto a clean tea towel, and squeeze out as much water as possible.

Chop the nettles finely.

Crush the toasted nuts or seeds using a mortar and pestle.

Add the garlic to the mortar and use the pestle to grind or pound together. Add the salt, cheese, and nettles and pound until ingredients are evenly mixed.

Add the olive oil a tablespoon at a time, stirring to combine, until the pesto reaches the desired consistency.

SPRING SHOOTS

Cream of Nettle Soup

Sylvie Mitford, co-owner and head chef, The Boreal Diner, Bonavista

3 tbsp unsalted butter
6 shallots, diced finely
1 carrot, diced finely
2 stalks celery, diced finely
3 cloves garlic, minced
½ cup dry white wine or 2 tbsp apple cider vinegar
1 potato, peeled and diced
1 lb young tender stinging nettles, washed but not dried, leaves picked from stems (*wear gloves!*)
Vegetable stock
1–2 cups heavy cream
Salt and pepper
Lemon juice
Nutmeg

Melt the butter in a large heavy saucepan over a medium-low heat. Add the shallots, carrot, and celery. Sauté, stirring frequently, until the shallots are translucent, about 7 to 10 minutes. Add the garlic and cook another 2 to 3 minutes. Add the wine or vinegar and turn the heat to high. Scrape the browned bits of vegetables off the bottom of the pan as the wine boils.

When the wine has almost completely evaporated, turn the heat to low. Add the nettles and stir frequently; the water on the leaves should help steam and wilt the nettles slightly. When the nettles are wilted, add enough vegetable stock to come about two-thirds of the way up the nettles. Add the potato.

Cover the pot and bring to a boil. Reduce the heat and simmer for 10 minutes, or until the potato is tender. Remove from the heat and carefully blend until smooth with an immersion blender.

Add cream (as desired, depending on how thick or rich a soup you want), and salt and pepper to taste. Add a teaspoon or two of fresh lemon juice for a little zing. A pinch of freshly ground nutmeg is nice, too.

SPRING SHOOTS

SPRING SHOOTS

WINTERCRESS

Wild mustard, bittercress, herb of St. Barbara
Barbarea vulgaris

 May - July

WHAT IS IT?

Wintercress is a biennial herb with a basal rosette of lobed, shiny, dark green leaves; plants produce an upright stem to 1 metre tall in their second year. Four-petalled yellow flowers are in clusters atop the stems.

Wintercress are abundant in disturbed areas, including vegetable gardens, gravel lots, and roadsides.

HOW TO HARVEST

Watch for wintercress leaves soon after snowmelt in the spring; it is one of the first plants to emerge, ready to harvest. During winters with little snow, this plant may be found even before spring arrives.

Pick greens and clusters of flowers.

HOW TO USE

Leaves can be eaten raw when collected in early spring: add to salads or sandwiches. Steam flower buds and serve with butter.

Leaves become bitter as the plants flower, although boiling (with one or two changes of water) removes most of the bitterness, leaving a sweet, mustardy flavour. Clusters of flower heads can also be boiled (change the water at least once) and served as you would broccoli.

SPRING SHOOTS

SPRING SHOOTS

YARROW

Thousandleaf
Achillea millefolium

WHAT IS IT?

Yarrow is also called thousandleaf or little feather, given its distinctive delicate, alternate, fern- or feather-like leaves. The stem is round and smooth; clusters of tiny white or pale pink-purple flowers bloom in midsummer. It is often short, just 15 to 20 centimetres tall, but can reach up to 80 centimetres in rich soil.

Yarrow is abundant in lawns, gravel lots, and other disturbed areas, including roadsides and sidewalk cracks.

HOW TO HARVEST

Pick the feathery greens in early spring until flowers emerge—then harvest the flowers. Yarrow has a long flowering season, making them ideal for flower arrangements.

HOW TO USE

Yarrow is an excellent fresh green if you catch it early in the spring—use it in salads, sandwiches, or as a herb in soup or pickles (I use yarrow, along with alder catkins, in Japanese knotweed pickles). Leaves become too bitter to eat when the plant flowers.

Make tea from fresh or dried yarrow flowers.

SPRING SHOOTS

Banks & Shores
Barrens
Clearings
Disturbed Areas
Forest
Wetlands

EAT YOUR WEEDS

The best way to get back at weeds is to eat them.

I worked as a gardener and landscaper for most of my teenage years and into my 20s. Over time I became aware of, and more and more interested in, the free food I was busily removing from people's property. In fact, many of the "weeds" I frantically removed from around precious annuals, perennials, and vegetables are not only edible but also delicious and packed with nutrients.

This section contains some of the most common summer weeds you'll see in lawns, flower and vegetable gardens, and gravel pits and near roads and other disturbed areas. I encourage everyone to learn which ones are edible—and enjoy the bounty.

As always, be aware of where you're picking. Urban lawns and flower gardens may be treated with pesticides or herbicides, or the soil may be high in lead or other contaminants, making these weeds unsuitable for eating.

EAT YOUR WEEDS

EAT YOUR WEEDS

CHICKWEED

Stellaria media

 June - November

WHAT IS IT?

Chickweed is found in the rich soil of vegetable gardens and flower beds, as well as in meadows, fields, and compost heaps and along roadsides and other disturbed areas. Opposite oval-shaped pointed leaves grow in pairs along the length of thin trailing stems. Tiny white flowers (0.5 centimetres in diameter or less) are star-shaped, with five deeply lobed petals. Plants grow in thick mats or clusters. Its leaves close at night or when rain is imminent; blossoms open late in the morning.

Chickens love chickweed—that's where the common name comes from.

HOW TO HARVEST

New chickweed plants emerge from mid-June until the snow falls. Harvest the entire above-ground plant by hand or with clippers.

HOW TO USE

Chickweed has a mild peppery flavour, similar to young spinach, and is a similar nutrient powerhouse. Use as a microgreen for sandwiches or salads all season long. Boil or steam chickweed and serve as a side dish.

EAT YOUR WEEDS

LAMB'S QUARTER

Goosefoot, wild spinach, wild quinoa
Chenopodium album L.

June - October

WHAT IS IT?

Lamb's quarter spreads quickly in a variety of habitats, including gardens, beaches, compost piles, roadsides, and other disturbed areas. Plants are usually 30 to 50 centimetres tall but can reach 1 metre. Its waxy toothed leaves are an elongated diamond shape. Younger leaves appear powdery or sugar-coated. Clustered greenish flowers develop a red hue at maturity and produce round seeds.

Frequently called wild spinach or goosefoot (for the shape of the leaves), Lamb's quarter is actually related to quinoa (*Chenopodium quinoa*).

HOW TO HARVEST

Collect young shoots or leaves in the spring; look for plants that are 15 centimetres long or less for the best salad greens. Pick the tender leaf tips all season long.

Harvest flowers in the fall, when they turn reddish.

HOW TO USE

Leaves have a pleasant nutty, spinach-like taste and are a great addition to a wild green salad. Greens harvested later in the summer are better suited to cooked dishes than salads. Steam, add to stir-fries or soups, or blanch and store for winter use.

Treat the flower as you would quinoa: boil in water until tender, drain, and serve as porridge or a side dish, or toast in the oven.

Lamb's quarter leaves contain some oxalic acid and should be consumed in moderation. Cooking removes this acid. Seeds contain saponins, which may be mildly toxic and should not be consumed in excess.

EAT YOUR WEEDS

Banks & Shores
Barrens
Clearings
Disturbed Areas
Forest
Wetlands

Lamb's Quarter and Brown Quinoa Porridge

Kyle Puddester, chef, Fork Restaurant, Mobile

½ cup lamb's quarter grain
1 cup lamb's quarter leaves
2 cups brown quinoa
2 cups chicken stock, heated in a separate pot
1 large onion, small dice
1 cup mixed wild mushrooms (chanterelles, hedgehogs, etc.)
8 cloves garlic, minced
1 tbsp fresh thyme, chopped
½ cup white wine
1 cup Parmesan cheese, grated
½ cup heavy cream
½ cup butter + ¼ cup cold butter

Rinse the leaves and allow to dry on paper towel. Spread the grains on a baking sheet and place in the oven on the lowest setting for 30 minutes to dry. Once dry, allow to cool and then transfer the grains into a fine mesh strainer and shake. This will remove the husk, leaving a small, dark-coloured grain.

In a large rondeau pot (or Dutch oven), heat ½ cup butter until melted and frothy. Add the onion and mushrooms and sauté until caramelized. Add the garlic and thyme and cook until fragrant. Add the lamb's quarter grains and quinoa and stir to coat. Deglaze the pan with white wine and cook until the liquid has almost completely evaporated. Slowly add the hot chicken stock, a cup at a time, allowing the liquid to evaporate after each addition.

To finish, add the cream and Parmesan and allow the cream to reduce by half. Remove the pan from the heat. Stir in the lamb's quarter leaves and the cold butter. Season with salt and pepper.

Kyle Puddester and Kayla O'Brien, Fork. See Kayla's recipe, page 238.

EAT YOUR WEEDS

PENNYCRESS

Field pennycress
Thlaspi arvense

WHAT IS IT?

Pennycress, a member of the mustard family, is a hairless annual frequently found along roadsides and in other disturbed areas. The plant has two forms: with upright stems to 60 centimetres tall, or with stems growing as a mat along the ground. Toothed arrow-shaped leaves grow the length of the upright stem. Small white flowers are in spikes; each 3-millimetre-diameter bloom has four petals. Later in the season pennycress has 1-centimetre-diameter flat, round-to-oval pods with two ears.

HOW TO HARVEST

Pick young leaves before the plant flowers. Leaves become very bitter later in the season.

HOW TO USE

Pennycress leaves have a sharp mustard flavour. Chop young leaves and add raw to a salad, or steam.

EAT YOUR WEEDS

EAT YOUR WEEDS

EAT YOUR WEEDS

PINEAPPLEWEED

Wild chamomile
Matricaria discoidea

June - September

WHAT IS IT?
Pineappleweed is a robust and widespread plant, frequently seen growing through cracks in pavement and sidewalks, along roadsides and paths, as well as in gardens and other disturbed areas. A low-growing (to 30 centimetres) relative of the aster family, pineappleweed resembles its close relative chamomile in appearance, without the white petals. Flower heads are green to yellow and cone-shaped. Leaves are feathery and finely divided.

To identify this plant, rub a flower bud and smell. If you detect the aroma of pineapple, you are holding pineappleweed.

HOW TO HARVEST
Pick plants all summer long, when its flower buds emerge.

Many choose to harvest or eat only the flower heads; these can be picked by hand or removed with clippers.

HOW TO USE
Pineappleweed is an excellent find for people who are allergic to pineapple but enjoy the taste. It's my favourite wild plant for tea or flavoured water. Most mornings before I go foraging, I pack my water bottle with pineappleweed, fill it with fresh water, and go.

Pineappleweed can be used in many dessert recipes for a similar sweet flavour. Use to make a tropical ice cream.

Use fresh or dried flower heads and leaves to make tea. Add fresh flower heads to salads or use to make jelly or a simple syrup for cocktails. Dry the flower heads and crush with sea salt for a fish spice.

EAT YOUR WEEDS

Toasted Milk Pineappleweed Cream and Strawberries

Celeste Mah, pastry chef, Raymonds Restaurant

This is a super easy, super delicious dessert for the summer.

500 ml heavy cream
50 g skim milk powder
50 g sugar
A big handful of pineappleweed (leaves, flowers, stems)

Put the milk powder in a small saucepan and slowly toast over a low heat. Make sure to stir it once in a while as it warms. When it starts toasting, stir continuously so that it doesn't stick to the bottom of the pan and burn.

Add the cream and sugar to the toasted powder and stir with a whisk until everything is combined. Add the pineappleweed and bring the entire mixture to the point the cream is almost to a boil.

Remove the pan from the heat, cover, and let stand to infuse the cream with the pineappleweed. When the mixture has cooled, strain through a fine mesh strainer and chill overnight.

When you are ready to use the cream, whip with a mixer and whisk attachment to medium-stiff peaks. Serve with cut strawberries tossed with a pinch of sugar.

Celeste Mah.

EAT YOUR WEEDS

PLANTAIN

Wild plantain, broadleaf plantain
Plantago major

WHAT IS IT?

Plantain is a perennial immediately identifiable by its spike of compact flowers—about the size, shape, and colour of a pencil—arising from its basal leaves. Its flower stems are erect and hairless; individual flowers are tiny (2 to 3 millimetres in diameter), four-petalled, greenish, and stalkless.

Its thick egg-shaped leaves grow in a rosette. Leaves are 5 to 30 centimetres long; each has five to seven parallel visible veins. Plants are up to 15 centimetres tall.

Although this plant shares a name with plantain fruit, the two are unrelated.

HOW TO HARVEST

Harvest leaves early in the season; they quickly become tough and fibrous. Collect flowers into the fall.

HOW TO USE

Eat young leaves raw in a salad; steam or blanch older leaves before adding to soups and stews. Leaves will become too tough to eat later in the season.

Plantain is useful all season long as a poultice to soothe insect or nettle stings or sunburns. Simply chew the leaves and place on the affected area.

Plantain flowers can be used as an egg substitute in baking. Separate the flowers from the stalk and place in a bowl. Cover with water and allow to sit until the mixture becomes gelatinous.

EAT YOUR WEEDS

75

EAT YOUR WEEDS

SHEPHERD'S PURSE

Capsella bursa-pastoris

May - July

WHAT IS IT?

Fuzzy shepherd's purse leaves emerge in early spring. A stem reaching 50 centimetres grows upright from a rosette of lobed leaves. A few pointed leaves grow singly from the stem; tiny white four-petalled flowers (0.25 centimetres in diameter or smaller) are followed by heart-shaped seed pods (the "purse" of this plant's common name).

Shepherd's purse, a member of the mustard family, is common in vegetable gardens and grassy disturbed areas.

HOW TO HARVEST

Pick the first leaves in early spring; flowers usually emerge by mid-June. The entire plant can be eaten.

Pick seed pods later in the summer.

HOW TO USE

Shepherd's purse has a mild radish–cabbage taste. Add leaves, flowers, and seed pods to salads. Eat the entire plant raw on a sandwich, steam, or add to stews or soups.

Collect seeds to use as a spice (similar to mustard seed) or to sprout. Roots can be dried, eaten fresh, or cooked.

EAT YOUR WEEDS

EAT YOUR WEEDS

Garden sorrel.

Curly dock.

EAT YOUR WEEDS

SORREL + CURLY DOCK

Sheep sorrel, garden sorrel, curly dock
Rumex acetosella, Rumex acetosa, Rumex crispus

May – November

WHAT IS IT?

Three types of sorrel are widespread throughout Newfoundland: sheep sorrel, garden sorrel, and curly dock. All are perennial introduced species.

Both sheep sorrel and garden sorrel have arrow-shaped leaves, with two lobes where the main part of the leaf meets the stem. Sheep sorrel is smaller and more compact, growing to about 30 centimetres in height; garden sorrel can reach almost twice that height. Round, reddish flowers grow in clusters along the stem. Sheep sorrel is the more flavourful of the two.

Curly dock resembles a scrawny rhubarb plant in appearance (the two species are in the same family); it has rhubarb-like thick leaves with curled edges and a coarse texture. Curly dock can grow to 1 metre or taller. Large clusters of pale green flowers grow on tall stalks; flowers turn into red-brown winged seeds in late summer.

HOW TO HARVEST

Look for all three species in meadows, as well as in gravel lots, fields, gardens, and other disturbed areas. Sheep sorrel can be tedious to harvest in disturbed areas; it tends to be most bountiful in cutovers.

Collect the leaves of all three species in the spring. Continue to harvest sorrel leaves until first frost; they send up new shoots all season. Curly dock leaves are only worth harvesting in spring when leaves are the most tender; pick them before or as they are unfurling.

Harvest curly dock seeds in late summer–early fall when they turn red-brown. The seeds, which grow in large clusters, can be collected by the handful.

EAT YOUR WEEDS

Curly dock.

Sheep sorrel.

Sheep sorrel.

Sheep sorrel.

EAT YOUR WEEDS

Garden sorrel.

HOW TO USE

Add sorrel leaves to salads, soups, and other dishes for a tart lemon taste. Add a handful of sorrel leaves to Caesar salads or cod au gratin (layer on top of the cod and white sauce instead of using lemon.

The Grounds Café (Murray's Garden Centre, Portugal Cove-St. Philip's) serves a sorrel "lemonade" to guests of our foraging tours. To make the drink, steep sorrel leaves in hot water. Add sugar or honey to taste, let cool, and serve over ice. Use dried sorrel leaves for a pink-coloured beverage.

Steam the leaves of garden sorrel or curly dock and serve with butter. Curly dock leaves are often boiled with, and served alongside, salt meat.

Dehydrate sorrel leaves for tea or to use as a spice. Combine dried sorrel leaves with dried Scotch lovage, spruce tips, and Newfoundland sea salt for a fish spice.

Toast curly dock seeds lightly in a small amount of oil and use in granola or porridge, or as a salad garnish.

Note: Sorrel and curly dock leaves have a sharp citrus taste, in part due to the presence of oxalic acid. All should be consumed in moderation.

EAT YOUR WEEDS

Sorrel and Mushroom Risotto

Chris Mercer, head chef, Brewdock; owner, Bandolero Sauces

4 L vegetable stock
8 stalks asparagus
60 g + 40 g fresh sorrel
½ yellow onion, diced
2 cloves garlic, diced
1 lemon
100 g grated Asiago cheese
3 tbsp unsalted butter
300 g arborio rice
2 oz white wine
300 g mushrooms of your choice, sliced
Oil (canola or olive, whatever's on hand)
Salt and pepper to taste

Bring the vegetable stock to a simmer in a medium saucepan and reduce the heat to the lowest setting.

Remove the tough bottom stem from the asparagus and drop into the simmering stock for 2 to 3 minutes or until softened. Remove asparagus from the stock.

Place cooked asparagus and 60 grams of sorrel in a blender or food processor with a splash of water and a pinch of salt. Blend or process until smooth and set aside.

In a wide heavy bottom frying pan, combine onions and garlic with a small amount of oil and place on medium-low heat. Add a pinch of salt.

Add the arborio rice to the pan and raise the heat slightly to medium. Stir the rice for 2 to 3 minutes until toasted and beginning to turn translucent. Add the white wine and let the mixture cook down for 1 minute.

Using a ladle, add hot vegetable stock to the rice, two ladlefuls at a time, and stir in. As the stock begins to soak into the rice after 1 to 2

EAT YOUR WEEDS

minutes of cooking, add more. Continue this process, stirring constantly until much of the stock has been used (you may not use it all).

Once you have added stock six to eight times and the rice tastes nearly cooked, add the mushrooms. If the rice is cooked to your liking, reduce the heat to low and stir in the asparagus and sorrel purée, butter, Asiago, a squirt of lemon juice, and the remaining 40 grams of sorrel. Stir vigorously until everything is incorporated; add salt and pepper if needed, and serve.

EAT YOUR WEEDS

STONECROP

Sedum
Sedum spp.

# May - August

WHAT IS IT?

This flowering succulent perennial is hardy and popular in flower gardens. Stonecrop is not a wild plant but it escapes cultivation easily and is often found in meadows and near old homesteads, foundations, and fruit trees. Large flower heads develop in late summer and mature to a deep pink in fall.

There are hundreds of sedum species; avoid harvesting yellow-flowering species.

HOW TO HARVEST

Start picking stonecrop shoots in late May–early June. Unlike many plants, you can harvest stonecrop leaves all season long, though they do become bitter as they mature. Do not harvest stonecrop with yellow flowers—you may need to wait a season to harvest to be sure which species you have found.

Before harvesting from any garden, ensure that no pesticides or chemicals were used on the plant or its soil.

HOW TO USE

Stonecrop has a fresh cucumber-like, slightly peppery, taste. Use the leaves in salad or stir-fries. Steam the leaves or the entire shoot.

EAT YOUR WEEDS

EAT YOUR WEEDS

Roast Lamb with Stonecrop, Caramelized Honey, and Tzatziki

Matthew Swift, head chef, Terre Restaurant, St. John's

As a kid, I was always having to weed sedum out of the garden—they are nice ornamental plants, but since they can generally grow anywhere, they do, and can be a bit invasive. The red flowering varieties are safe to eat raw; the yellow need to be cooked to avoid an upset stomach (early in the year it can be tough to tell the difference; if you are unsure, you may want to cook them all or wait until they bloom in the late summer).

As an adult, I was pleasantly surprised when I was told that these plants were good to eat. Their semi-succulent leaves are a great texture for salads, and the light bitterness and "green" taste means they hold up well and contrast with a variety of flavours and textures. We like to use them with grilled meats or roasted fish dishes. For the dish below, hot roast or grilled lamb works, but it is also delicious as a salad the next day with leftover cold roast.

Serves 4

750 g–1 kg lamb leg
Leaves from several stonecrop stalks
1/3 cup honey
2 tbsp butter
Olive oil
Sea salt
Tzatziki (recipe below)

Make the tzatziki and refrigerate.

Season and roast the lamb to your liking. For a piece this size, just over 1 hour at 375°F (190°C) should be about right. Let the roast rest 15 minutes.

In another pan, heat the honey over a medium heat and watch carefully. As the honey comes to a dark caramel (rich brown, but not

EAT YOUR WEEDS

black), add the butter and stir to combine. Add a few drops of water and any lamb drippings.

Brush the lamb with the honey, reserving some to sauce the plate.

Toss the stonecrop leaves with a little oil and sea salt.

Plate the tzatziki first. Slice the lamb and add to the plate; top with the dressed stonecrop leaves. Drizzle with the remaining caramelized honey, and serve.

Tzatziki
1 cup plain yogurt
1 small cucumber, or about 1/3 English cucumber
1 small clove garlic, microplaned (use more/less according to your taste)
Zest and juice of one lemon
½ bunch dill, chopped
½ bunch mint, chopped
Salt and pepper to taste

Grate and salt the cucumber. Let sit for 10 minutes in a colander to remove the water.

Combine all the ingredients and refrigerate until ready to use.

BEACH GREENS

Beach greens tend to be tough, hardy plants. They grow among the rocks and sand, usually just beyond the high-tide mark. These plants can handle being battered by wind and waves, and many taste salty from the ocean spray and the soil's salinity.

Many of these beach greens start early and last all summer. Beach peas, for example, emerge late in the spring and many are suitable for harvesting throughout the summer.

Most of these greens are perfect for using fresh in a salad, steamed or sautéed as a side dish, or as pot herbs. Then there's strand wheat, ready to be ground and added to your favourite baking recipe.

BEACH GREENS

BEACH GREENS

BEACH PEA

Lathyrus japonicus

May - September

WHAT IS IT?
Beach peas are wild peas that grow along the tide line or at the edges of rocky or sandy beaches. They resemble the pea plants you might see in a vegetable garden: they grow as vines, have compound leaves with three to seven pairs of leaflets with tendrils at the tip, and produce green pods of edible peas. Unlike garden peas, however, beach peas grow along the ground in tangled mats.

Its pink and purple flowers are about 2 centimetres long and grow in an unbrached cluster, or raceme.

HOW TO HARVEST
Harvest shoots when they are light green and tender. As the season progresses, plants become tougher, less pleasant to eat, and resistant to cutting.

Pick the flowers and ripe pods. As the pods are the same colour as the leaves, you may have to look closely to find them.

HOW TO USE
Beach pea shoots have a fresh green-pea flavour and are suitable for salads. Use flowers in salads or as a garnish.

Later in the season, shell peas, boil, and serve with butter.

BEACH GREENS

BEACH GREENS

GOOSETONGUE

Seaside plantain
Plantago maritima

May - September

WHAT IS IT?
Seaside plantain, a relative of the common plantain (*Plantago major*, page 74), has a similar upright cylinder of tightly packed flowers. Seaside plantain's leaves, however, are long, narrow, and grasslike.

Plants grow in clumps along the tide line, on gravel and rocky slopes, and in cliff cracks.

HOW TO HARVEST
Harvest the greens throughout the growing season, usually from late May into November. Snip only a few from each plant and leave the flowers.

HOW TO USE
Chop small tender leaves for salad greens. Steam longer/older leaves and serve with butter and black pepper.

Larger leaves are also suitable for pickling.

BEACH GREENS

ORACH

Atriplex glabriuscula, Atriplex patula

May - August

WHAT IS IT?

Orach resembles its relative lamb's quarter: both have wiry, branched, upright stems, spinach-like leaves, and clusters of red fruit. Orach can be distinguished by its arrowhead-shaped leaves; lamb's quarter leaves are generally more diamond-shaped.

Bright pink flowers emerge in late summer.

HOW TO HARVEST

Pick leaves all summer, until the plant goes to seed.

HOW TO USE

Orach is generally pleasantly salty but can be bitter. It is better steamed or boiled or used as a pot herb than as a salad green.

BEACH GREENS

Banks & Shores
Barrens
Clearings
Disturbed Areas
Forest
Wetlands

95

BEACH GREENS

BEACH GREENS

OYSTERLEAF

Sea lungwort, sea bluebells
Mertensia maritima

WHAT IS IT?
Oysterleaf is another shoreside plant that grows along the tide line on rocky and gravel-like beaches. It is especially common on Newfoundland's Southern Shore. Oysterleaf is overall matte light bluish-green, with round- to oval-shaped leaves. Its leaves are thick, resembling those of a succulent.

The stems reach 30 centimetres. The flowers are bluish purple and pink and grow in clusters.

HOW TO HARVEST
Don't pick the whole plant. Just take some of the leaves and flowers, leaving the root and some of the green. You can harvest the leaves from spring to the end of the season.

Be gentle when harvesting; leaves bruise easily.

HOW TO USE
Oysterleaf leaves taste like a west-coast oyster. Chop and use in a salad, or steam. Flowers and leaves can be pickled and are a perfect addition to a charcuterie board.

THE FORAGER'S DINNER

BEACH GREENS

ROSEROOT

Rhodiola rosea

May - June

WHAT IS IT?
Roseroot is in the sedum family and resembles stonecrop in appearance. Thick, fleshy, waxy greyish green leaves grow from stiff, upright stems. Vibrant yellow flowers form at the end of each stalk.

Roseroot grows in unusual places—on cliffs, in the cracks of rocks, and on exposed ledges.

HOW TO HARVEST
Roseroot does not grow in abundance on the Avalon Peninsula, so pick sparingly, if at all. It is common and widespread on the Bonavista Peninsula and elsewhere on the island.

Pick stems and leaves before the plant flowers. Leaves become unpalatably bitter after flowering.

HOW TO USE
Use as fresh salad greens, steam, or add to soups.

BEACH GREENS

BEACH GREENS

SANDWORT

Sea chickweed, sea sandwort
Honckenya peploides

May - September

WHAT IS IT?
Sandwort resembles garden chickweed but has waxier, thicker leaves. Plants grow in large patches or mats in the sand or among pebbles and rocks. Tiny white to green flowers have five deeply notched petals.

Plants quickly die after seeds are formed—note where you found it and watch for them to emerge the next spring. A second crop will often appear in late summer.

HARVEST
Cut plants at the base, leaving enough to flower and spread. Harvest and use the whole plant—stem, leaves, and first flowers—until seed pods emerge, when the plants become quite woody and bitter.

HOW TO USE
This is my favourite beach green, for its satisfying crunch, peppery flavour, and ocean-like aftertaste. Chop and add to a salad (try my beach-green coleslaw, page 103), steam, or pickle.

BEACH GREENS

Banks & Shores
Barrens
Clearings
Disturbed Areas
Forest
Wetlands

101

Beach Green Coleslaw

Shawn Dawson

For my Cod Wars entry during the 2019 Roots, Rants, and Roars food festival (Elliston, NL), I made wild mushroom cod au gratin with beach green coleslaw. You can prepare this salad right on the beach—it goes well with any boil-up.

2 handfuls sandwort
1 handful garden sorrel
1 handful flowering oysterleaf
1 handful sea rocket leaves

Rinse beach greens, chop, and place in a bowl. Prepare spruce tip vinaigrette and pour over the greens. Toss and serve.

<u>Spruce tip vinaigrette</u>
1 handful spruce tips
1 tbsp local honey
1 small clove garlic, minced or diced
Sea salt and pepper
Equal parts olive oil and apple cider vinegar

If you are using frozen spruce tips, take them out of the freezer and let thaw. When they have lost most of their moisture (or if you are using fresh spruce tips), chop finely. Place in a Mason jar along with the other ingredients. Shake until fully combined. Alternatively, use a blender to mix.

BEACH GREENS

BEACH GREENS

SCOTCH LOVAGE

Ligusticum scoticum

June - August

WHAT IS IT?
Those familiar with the garden herb lovage will immediately recognize scotch lovage. Its triangular compound leaves are bright green, stiff, and shiny. Plants grow 30 to 60 centimetres tall, in large patches. The stems are usually dark brown.

Clusters of small white flowers bloom in midsummer.

HOW TO HARVEST
Cut plants at the base until they go to seed, usually in midsummer. Harvest seeds into the fall.

HOW TO USE
Scotch lovage tastes like celery, parsley, and lovage and is excellent for flavouring soups, stews, and green or potato salads. Chop stems and leaves and add to a salad or steam. Incorporate Scotch lovage in butter.

Seeds resemble fenugreek in flavour and can be used as a spice.

BEACH GREENS

BEACH GREENS

Shawn's Love Butter
Shawn Dawson

4 tbsp butter
A small handful of Scotch lovage sprigs
Sea salt + pepper
Fresh lemon

Chop up the leaves from the lovage sprigs. Squeeze a little fresh lemon juice on the lovage to preserve the green colour.

Melt the butter in a pot. Add sea salt, pepper, and the Scotch lovage. Heat gently for five minutes to infuse a nice flavour of love throughout the butter.

Make this recipe on beach; it is perfect with fresh bread and mussels.

BEACH GREENS

SEA ROCKET

Cakile edentula

WHAT IS IT?

Sea rocket grows with or near oysterleaf and other beach greens. Sea rocket's unusual leaves are its distinguishing feature: bright green, thick, oblong, and broader toward the top, with rounded teeth along the edges.

Its four-petalled white flowers are followed by a cone-shaped fruit in late summer.

HOW TO HARVEST

Harvest the leaves and stems throughout the growing seasons. Don't pick the shoots and be sure to leave most of the plant to propagate.

HOW TO USE

Sea rocket has a strong wasabi taste. Add to salads and sandwiches or steam.

Pickle seed pods and add to cocktails.

“# BEACH GREENS

Banks & Shores
Barrens
Clearings
Disturbed Areas
Forest
Wetlands

BEACH GREENS

BEACH GREENS

STRAND WHEAT

Leymus arenarius
Ammophila breviligulata (American beachgrass)

June - September

WHAT IS IT?
These sturdy beach grasses grow 50 to 100 centimetres high and produce grain heads of about 15 centimetres in length. Its bladelike leaves are greyish green; mature grain heads are light brown.

HOW TO HARVEST
Harvest the mature grain.

HOW TO USE
Grind the grain for flour.

FRESHWATER WEEDS

Get your rubber boots on and get ready to make a mojito!

A range of tasty edibles, including a variety of mints, grows throughout Newfoundland in damp soil and along the edges of lakes, streams, rivers, and ponds.

In most cases, it's best to harvest the plant above the water's surface. And as always, be aware of where you're collecting. Never take plants from ditches, stagnant waters, or other polluted areas.

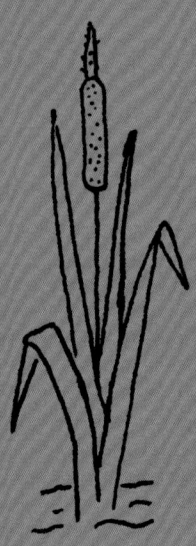

FRESHWATER WEEDS

CATTAILS

Bull rush, bog corn
Typha latifolia

 May - June

WHAT IS IT?

Cattails are tall (1.5–2 metres), water-loving perennials. Its leaves are grasslike. Male and female flowers are found on the same stalk: female flowers are tightly packed into a distinct, fuzzy hot-dog shape; male flowers form the spike above.

Cattails grow in roadside ditches, marshes, and bogs and along rivers, beaches, and shorelines. Cattails are sometimes planted to help remediate polluted areas—never harvest from a known polluted area.

HOW TO HARVEST

All parts of the cattail are edible. To harvest, start with a pair of rubber boots, hip waders if possible. The ground is often soft where cattails grow; be prepared to sink.

Shoots: Reach your hand into the water at the very base of the plant, loosen the roots, and pluck out the entire shoot when you feel the roots give way. Do not overharvest; you want to enjoy the flowers and pollen later in the season.

Flower: Harvest the flower while it is still green (enclosed by its papery sheath) by cutting the stalk just below the flower cluster.

Pollen: Place a paper bag over the flower head. Shake the plant to release the pollen into the bag. You may be surprised how much pollen you get.

Be sure to check plants for grubs. There are usually few to none when the plants are young but they proliferate as the plants mature.

FRESHWATER WEEDS

HOW TO USE

Young cattail shoots have a cucumber-celery flavour. Prepare like leeks, cutting back the green and using primarily the white sections. Stir-fry, roast, pickle, or eat raw.

Boil or roast the immature "hot dog" (be sure to harvest the flowers while they are still green) and eat like corn on the cob. Make cattail flower pickles.

Use the pollen as flour to thicken soups or stews, or use in baked goods.

Dry the roots and grind to make flour. The roots are also used as a source of starch.

Cattail leaves can be used in basket making.

THE FORAGER'S DINNER

FRESHWATER WEEDS

Ross Larkin.

Cattail Blini

Ross Larkin, chef de cuisine, Raymonds Restaurant

Blini are thin Russian and Ukrainian pancakes. Add savoury or sweet toppings of choice.

½ cup cattail pollen
½ cup all-purpose flour
2 tsp baking powder
1 cup homogenized milk
1 egg
Pinch of salt
1 tbsp white sugar

Mix the dry ingredients together. Add the wet ingredients. Mix well.

Place a pan on a medium-high heat, and wait for it to be as hot as possible on this setting. Do not add any oil to the pan.

Transfer the mixture into something that is able to pour a steady stream (I use a squeeze bottle). Squeeze or pour portions of the mixture into the pan. The blinis should be about 28 millimetres in diameter, just larger than a dollar coin.

Once in the pan, leave the blinis for a moment to cook away from the pan, then turn over. They will not take much time because of their small size.

FRESHWATER WEEDS
RIVER MINT

Mentha arvensis, Mentha cardiaca

May - October

WHAT IS IT?
River mint, a perennial herb that grows in abundance along riverbeds and the edges of ponds, is easily identified by its scent—gently rub a leaf and instantly you will know if you are holding mint.

Two types of mint are found wild in Newfoundland: wild mint and heart mint. Both have opposite leaves. Heart mint, which has purple stems and deep green leaves, is hairless. Wild mint is covered in short, stiff hairs and is a lighter green than heart mint. Bright pink-purple clusters of flowers form between the wild mint leaves.

HOW TO HARVEST
Clip young shoots at the base or, if growing in water, at the water's surface; leave the root system intact to ensure a continuous harvest. Later in the season, clip shorter pieces of stem from the top—there's no need to take the entire plant. Although the leaves thicken as they age, mint can be picked and used throughout the growing season. In the fall, cut mint plants from the base, tie in bunches, and hang to dry.

Harvest mint from clean, moving water, ideally from a clean stream or the edges of a pond.

HOW TO USE
Micro mint (the first shoots) is tender and ideal for a garnish, in salads or in cocktails. Use mint of all ages for tea or cocktails (mojitos especially). Make mint jelly to serve with moose or lamb.

Dried mint can be used for tea or seasoning.

FRESHWATER WEEDS

Banks & Shores
Barrens
Clearings
Disturbed Areas
Forest
Wetlands

FRESHWATER WEEDS

Moose Shank With Mint + Lovage

Lori McCarthy, Cod Sounds, St. John's

<u>Salsa verde</u>
1 tbsp red wine vinegar
¼ tsp salt
¼ tsp pepper
½ tsp Dijon mustard
1 tsp anchovy paste (or 2 anchovies mashed with a fork)
1 tsp capers, finely chopped
3 tbsp extra-virgin olive oil
2 tbsp freshly squeezed orange juice
Zest of one orange
½ tsp chili flakes or fresh red chili to taste (optional)

<u>Fresh herbs</u>
½ cup wild mint, finely chopped
½ cup wild Scotch lovage, finely chopped (parsley can be substituted)
¼ cup cilantro, finely chopped (optional)

4–6 moose shanks
Butter or sunflower oil
Salt and pepper
1 large onion, diced
2 cups moose or beef broth

Combine the salsa verde ingredients in a bowl. Add the fresh herbs and mix well. Make this no more than an hour before you are going to eat it.
    One of most important things you can do is taste the salsa verde once it is made. This recipe is to my taste and even I often add a little more vinegar or salt depending on my preferences at the moment. Taste and adjust to your own palate.
    In Newfoundland, moose shank meat is often cut off to use in ground moose, but when our moose is butchered, I ask for the shanks to

Lori McCarthy.

be cut in 2-inch horizontal rounds. This gives a good round of marrow in each slice. You'll need a long and slow braise for this recipe, so get out that slow cooker and, trust me, the shanks are worth the wait. Moose shanks offer the perfect balance of gelatin to meat, making them some of the best cuts on the moose and one of my favourites.

    Salt and pepper the shanks well on both sides. Sear them on the stovetop in batches to brown on both sides. Place directly into the slow cooker. Add the chopped onion and broth. Cover and let the shanks cook until they fall off the bone. This could take 4 to 6 hours on low. Freeze any leftover liquid ("liquid gold") for another use, then pull the meat and combine it well. This can be done well ahead of supper and simply put it back in the slow cooker until you're ready. Serve it nice and hot with salsa verde.

    This salsa verde makes a great topping for meat of any kind. I often use it on leftover roasted leg of lamb for a quick supper. Simply pull leftover meat to create a pulled-pork-like pile of meat, warm it up, and serve it piled high with salsa verde. Stuff in in a tortilla or serve over a salad.

FRESHWATER WEEDS

FRESHWATER WEEDS

WATERCRESS

Nasturtium microphyllum

WHAT IS IT?

Watercress is a hardy, fast-growing aquatic or semi-aquatic perennial found along the banks of streams and ponds and in ditches. Its creeping stems are hollow, which enables the plants to float at the water's surface, and up to 1 metre long. Its green, alternate, hairless leaves have three to nine lobes.

The four-petalled white flowers (0.5 centimetres in diameter) grow in clusters and develop into seed pods reaching 2.5 centimetres in length.

HOW TO HARVEST

Harvest only from clean, moving water. Plants emerge in mid-spring; harvest leaves above the waterline until plants flower. Seed pods are also edible.

HOW TO USE

Watercress leaves and seed pods have a sharp, peppery taste, similar to that of watercress, radish, or mustard, which are all relatives. Use in salads, sandwiches, stir-fries, or soups.

FRESHWATER WEEDS

WILD BASIL

Dogmint
Clinopodium vulgare.

WHAT IS IT?
Wild basil tastes nothing like cultivated basil, nor is it in the same family— it gets its common name because of its appearance; it does look like basil, but hairy. In fact, wild basil is related to the wild mints found in Newfoundland, though it is less common. Like those mints, wild basil plants are upright, with square stems and opposite deep green leaves. Its leaves and stems are covered in fine hairs.

A spike of pink-purple flowers blooms in late summer. Wild basil grows in damp soil, as well as on heaths.

HOW TO HARVEST
Cut wild basil plants just below the first set of leaves, as you would garden basil. This will allow the plant to continue to grow throughout the summer.

HOW TO USE
The oregano-mint flavour of wild basil makes it well suited to soups, stews, and cocktails.

Make tea from dried or fresh leaves.

FRESHWATER WEEDS

Banks & Shores

Barrens

Clearings

Disturbed Areas

Forest

Wetlands

125

SEAWEEDS

Seaweeds are fast-growing macroalgae found in abundance in the coastal waters of Newfoundland. They're also superfoods, rich in iodine, B vitamins, iron, and an array of other nutrients. Many seaweeds can also be harvested throughout the year, offering a winter foraging option (for those who can tolerate the cold).

When harvesting seaweed to eat, always cut fresh seaweeds. Don't take seaweed that has washed up on the beach, as tempting as that may be, except to add to your garden. Be cautious on slippery coastal rocks. The ideal time to harvest is during low tide, when you safely cut from the rocks—or put on your wetsuit and get in the ocean.

This section introduces five prevalent Newfoundland seaweeds. Seaweeds have a variety of uses: dry and grind seaweed as a salt substitute. Use to make seaweed butters, pickles, or salads. Add to soups, stews, and other cooked dishes for flavour.

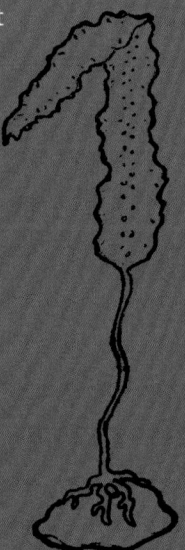

SEAWEEDS

SEAWEEDS

BLADDERWRACK

Black tang
Fucus vesiculosus

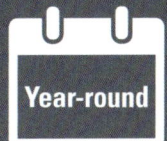

WHAT IS IT?

Bladderwrack fronds are about 2.5 centimetres wide, grow up to 1 metre in length, and have a distinct rib running up the centre of each. Prominent bubble-like air bladders are distinguishing features. Bladderwrack grows in abundance on the rocks, in shallow water along most of the coast of Newfoundland. It is delicious fried with garlic. Dry bladderwrack and steep for tea. This is the seaweed used to make a Seaweed Gose at Mill Street Brewery in St. John's.

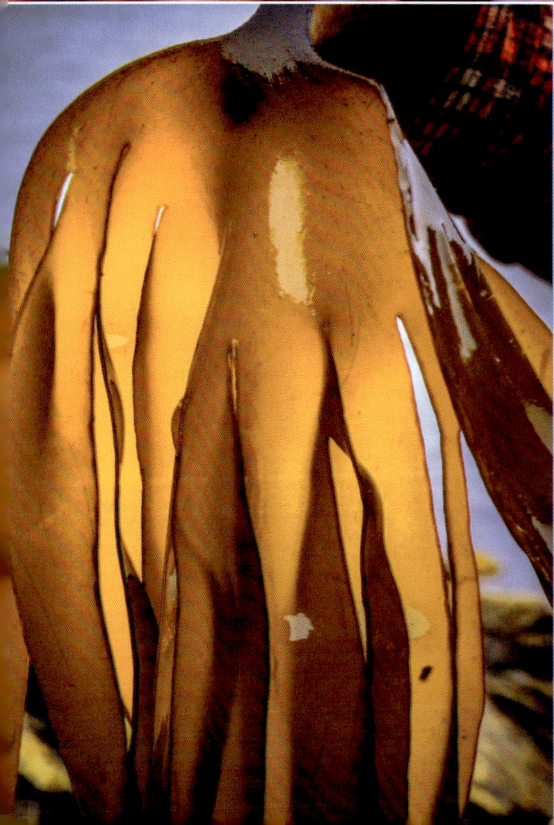

SEAWEEDS

SEAWEEDS

OARWEED

Laminaria digitata

Year-round

WHAT IS IT?
Oarweed fronds can be spotted floating on the ocean surface during low tide. Fronds grow to 2 to 3 metres in length, including a flexible stalk (about 2.5 centimetres in diameter) and a brown, broad blade, which is split into fingers. Fronds are attached to the seabed with tough, rootlike holdfasts. Among other uses, oarweed stalks make excellent pickles (see recipe on the next page); fronds can be used to make seaweed chips.

SEA OLIVES
Shawn Dawson

Makes 1 L pickles

1–3 freshly harvested oarweed stalks
½ inch fresh ginger, peeled and sliced
pinch chili flakes
1 cup apple cider vinegar
3/4 cup water

1 tbsp brown sugar
1 tsp juniper berries
1 red pepper, slices
Sea salt

Prepare jars
Sterilize jars by boiling in a pot of water for 10 minutes. Let dry.

Prepare seaweed
Never harvest seaweed that has washed up on the beach; always harvest it fresh at low tide. Slice the stalks to desired thickness. Wash slices well using a strainer, to remove as much of the gelatinous substance as you can.

Add flavour
Add chili flakes, sliced ginger, juniper berries, and red pepper to the jars.

Add sea olives
Pack oarweed into jars, leaving 1 centimetre or so of space at the top.

Make brine
Mix vinegar, water, and brown sugar in a saucepan over high heat. Bring to a boil, stirring occasionally, until the sugar dissolves.
   Pour brine into the jars to cover the oarweed. Refrigerate or process to seal for longer shelf life.

SEAWEEDS

SEAWEEDS
RED DULSE

Palmaria palmata

WHAT IS IT?

Red dulse, which grows from a disc-shaped holdfast attached to rocks or, often, oarweed stalks, has an inconspicuous stalk and leaflike fronds that vary in colour from deep pink to red-brown or purple. The texture is leather-like. Dried dulse is a popular snack worldwide.

SEAWEEDS

135

SEAWEEDS

SEA LETTUCE

Ulva lactuca

WHAT IS IT?
The salad green of sea vegetables, sea lettuce, like its common namesake, is light to dark green. Ruffle-edged leaflike fronds attach to rocks or other substrates with a disc-shaped holdfast. Sea lettuce is popularly eaten raw or added to soups. As it grows well in nutrient-rich waters, it is often abundant near outfalls—always check the surroundings before you harvest this, or any seaweed, to ensure that you are picking from clean water.

SEAWEEDS

SEAWEEDS

SEAWEEDS

SUGAR KELP

Sea belt
Laminaria saccharina, Saccharina latissima

Year-round

WHAT IS IT?
Sugar kelp fronds are brown-yellow and grow to 5 metres in length and up to 20 centimetres or more wide. The blades are long, wavy-edged ribbons and are attached to rocks by a short stalk and a root-like holdfast. Stalks are shorter than those of oarweed, and the blades are not divided, as oarweed blades are. Use in salads, soups, and stews, or roast or deep-fry.

SEAWEEDS

Seaweed Salad

Courtney and Terrence Howell, Grates Cove Studios, Grates Cove

STEP 1: Make ginger dressing

½ cup diced onion
1 large carrot
1 large stalk of celery, minced
2 tbsp water
4 tsp soy sauce
2 tsp lemon juice
¼ tsp ground black pepper
½ tsp Newfoundland Salt Company sea salt
½ cup vegetable oil
3 tbsp minced fresh ginger root
1/3 cup rice vinegar
1 ripe tomato, diced
2 tsp white sugar
½ tsp minced garlic
1½ tbsp sesame oil

Blend all ingredients in a food processor or blender to the desired consistency. We like it chunkier for added texture.

STEP 2: Prepare seaweed

½ pound freshly foraged thin leafed brown seaweed
   (we use a young saccharina)

Cut along the central stem to produce two long strips; compost the stem. Roll the long strips of seaweed tightly and cut across the grain to ½-centimetre (¼-inch) strips. Boil seaweed strips for 10 minutes or until tender but not mushy. Reserve 2 tbsp seaweed broth for marinade. Strain the seaweed and set aside to cool.

STEP 3: Make seaweed marinade

2 tbsp seaweed broth
1 tbsp rice vinegar
¼ tsp sesame oil
1 tsp miso paste
¼ to ½ tsp Bayou Bay Cajun
   Seasoning (optional)
1 tsp sugar
¼ tsp fresh lemon juice

Combine all ingredients.

SEAWEEDS

STEP 4: Bring it together
Add the cooled seaweed to the marinade. Refrigerate for 30 minutes. Remove seaweed from the marinade and place in a serving bowl. Add the desired amount of ginger dressing and mix. Garnish with freshly cut green onion and toasted sesame seeds. Top with local snow crab, if desired. Enjoy!

EAT THE TREES (AND SHRUBS)

Just like our fruit trees and berry bushes, Newfoundland's coniferous and deciduous trees and shrubs provide a great, if surprising, bounty of wild food.

From the citrus tang of spruce tips to peppery alder catkins, our trees have much to contribute to the local culinary experience.

EAT THE TREES (AND SHRUBS)

EAT THE TREES (AND SHRUBS)

ALDER

American green alder, speckled alder
Alnus spp.

October - June

WHAT IS IT?

Alder, a widespread deciduous shrub that grows to 3 metres tall, is found in almost all habitats throughout Newfoundland: in forests, along highways and other roadsides, beside rivers and ponds, and on rocky slopes. It is among the first and most prevalent shrubs to appear in regenerating disturbed areas.

Dark green, alternate, and oval alder leaves have serrated edges and grow from 4 to 8 centimetres in length. Male and female alder catkins (petal-less flower clusters) grow on the same tree: female catkins are hard, cone-shaped, and shorter than male catkins. Female catkins are bright green in summer and brown and woody in fall and winter. Male catkins are tight, pendulous, resinous green-brown aromatic buds that look like hanging caterpillars in late spring.

American green alder is the species most often found throughout the province; speckled alder is widepread and common in western and central Newfoundland.

HOW TO HARVEST

Male catkins can be harvested throughout the winter and early spring. The bark and branches can be harvested any time for smoking; they are more potent in winter than spring.

Male catkins have a great deal of resin and your fingers may quickly become sticky when picking them. Use cooking oil to remove the resin from your fingers.

EAT THE TREES (AND SHRUBS)

EAT THE TREES (AND SHRUBS)

HOW TO USE

Dry catkins and grind them to make alder pepper. Harvest bark and branches, age, and use to smoke meats and fish. Dry the inner bark and grind to use as flour.

For a Forager's Dinner event, Jon Howse (Fixed Coffee, St. John's) and I infused olive oil with alder catkins. We served this delicious, faintly floral oil with mussels. The Newfoundland Salt Company produces a finishing salt with roasted alder buds, a perfect pairing with white fish or other protein.

THE FORAGER'S DINNER

EAT THE TREES (AND SHRUBS)

BALSAM FIR

Abies balsamea

WHAT IS IT?
This native evergreen conifer is widespread and common in Newfoundland, often growing near spruce trees. Its leaves are flat needles up to 3 centimetres long; they are dark green on top with white bands on the underside. To distinguish a fir tree from a white or black spruce, look at the needles: spruce needles are square, while fir needles are flat and difficult to roll between your fingers.

Fir needles are high in vitamin C.

HOW TO HARVEST
Harvest the bright green tender tips at the ends of tree branches in the spring by snapping them off. As these "fir tips" are the tree's new growth, harvest only a handful or two per tree. See spruce (page 163) for more details—fir tips and spruce tips are similar in taste and use.

Fir tips are not as flavourful as spruce tips but they are still quite aromatic.

HOW TO USE
Use as you would spruce tips (page 165). Balsam fir is also popular as an essential oil. The pitch can be chewed like gum.

EAT THE TREES (AND SHRUBS)

EAT THE TREES (AND SHRUBS)

EAT THE TREES (AND SHRUBS)

BIRCH

Betula spp.

May - June

WHAT IS IT?
A number of birch species are found in Newfoundland, especially throughout central Newfoundland and on the island's west coast.

Birch are thin-leaved deciduous trees known for their white, papery bark and valuable hardwood. Their leaves are serrated, alternate, and often appear in pairs. Delicate flowers appear in three-flowered clusters before or as the leaves emerge.

HOW TO HARVEST
Pick male catkins while they are still closed and hard.

Birch trees can be tapped in the same way as maple trees are (see page 158). Birch-tapping season generally follows the maple-tapping season, beginning in late April or early May.

HOW TO USE
Use birch catkins as you would alder: dehydrate, crush, and use to flavour salads, meats, and cooked vegetable dishes.

Birch water (birch sap) is a refreshing, slightly sweet, drink that can be consumed straight out of the tree. Use birch water to make birch beer—simply replace the water used in fermentation with birch water.

Make birch syrup, about half the sweetness of maple syrup, by boiling down the birch water.

EAT THE TREES (AND SHRUBS)

JUNIPER

Common juniper, ground juniper
Juniperus communis

Year-round

WHAT IS IT?
Common juniper is a sprawling, low-growing coniferous evergreen shrub in the cedar family. It has dense, sharp needles up to 2 centimetres long. Juniper bushes are usually found close to the ocean, on rocky hillsides and barrens, along cliffs, and in other exposed areas.

Juniper "berries" are actually female cones, which gradually change from white or green to a deep purple-blue. Ripening can take two to three years.

HOW TO HARVEST
Pick the berries after they have turned dark. Picking and cleaning berries in large quantities can be labour-intensive due to the many small, prickly needles on the bush.

HOW TO USE
Juniper berries, known for giving gin its distinctive taste, dehydrate in a few days in an open bowl or tray placed in a dry, warm area. They can then be used as a pickling spice, crushed with sea salt, or stored in a sealed glass jar for future use.

Juniper berries are also a perfect flavouring for lamb or wild game—add a handful to the pan while roasting the meat. They can also be pickled, capered, or added to soups and stews.

Juniper branches are aromatic; add a few branches to the BBQ or smoker when smoking fish, meat, or peppers.

EAT THE TREES (AND SHRUBS)

EAT THE TREES (AND SHRUBS)

Juniper Smoked Lamb

Colin Moïse, chef and forager, owner of Renegade Harvest, Toronto

I was introduced to Andrew Thornly of Campbellton Berry Farm through a mutual friend. I've always supported the local food economy no matter where I am. As proud as I am of Andrew's farming practices, I was peculiarly interested in Campbellton Berry Farm's lamb and farm animals.

This recipe is inspired by Andrew's lamb. Lamb chops are quickly smoked with juniper and crowberry shrubbery. It needs a quick but hard smoke. Starting with a bed of birch coals, add green sprigs to make a thick smoke, coating the exterior of the meat. This is followed by a simple seasoning of salt and pepper.

My choice for accompaniment is a juniper and brown butter sauce with a balsamic reduction as its base. Also, since we are in the realm of root vegetables, I showcase celery root as the lamb's co-star.

Juniper + balsamic vinegar syrup
4 oz butter
300 ml balsamic vinegar
1 clove garlic
Bay leaf
2 tsp black pepper
74 ml sugar
3 tbsp juniper berries
2 tbsp mustard seed
½ tsp salt

Celery root hash
2 cups celery root, grated
3 tbsp butter
2 cloves garlic
2 tbsp cream cheese
Salt pepper
Oil

EAT THE TREES (AND SHRUBS)

EAT THE TREES (AND SHRUBS)

LABRADOR TEA

Rhododendron groenlandicum

May - July

WHAT IS IT?

Labrador tea is a widespread and common shrub in the Rhododendron family found in bogs and other peatlands and in damp woods and clearings. Shrubs grow to 1 metre tall and have oblong oval leaves that are dark green and wrinkled on top, with a prominent central vein. Leaf undersides are distinctively covered with a thick collection of orange or rust-coloured hairs (this distinguishes Labrador tea from its toxic look-alike and neighbour, sheep laurel).

Clusters of bright white flowers appear in mid- to late summer.

HOW TO HARVEST

Pick leaves in early spring. Pick only a few from each plant to ensure its best chance of survival.

HOW TO USE

The leaves are used to make tea. Add to soups and stews for flavouring; be sure to add near the end of cooking and do not subject to high heat.

Important: do not boil the leaves, as doing so releases a harmful toxin (andromedotoxin). Bring water to a boil, remove from the heat, and steep leaves for several minutes.

EAT THE TREES (AND SHRUBS)

EAT THE TREES (AND SHRUBS)

MAPLE
Norway maple, sycamore maple, red maple, mountain maple
Acer spp.

March - April

WHAT IS IT?

Although sugar maples are not found in Newfoundland, any of the local maple trees can be tapped to collect sap for maple syrup. Local maple trees all have distinctive maple leaf-shaped leaves. Small yellow, green, white, or (in the case of red maple) red flowers appear in late spring; clusters of maple keys or samaras develop later in the season.

Mountain maple, the smallest of the listed species, often grows in forests and clearings. Mountain and red maple are native species to the province; sycamore and the more popular Norway maple are introduced but have spread from urban properties to roadsides and disturbed areas.

Maple sap is stored in the roots and transferred to the tips of the branches to enable it to leaf out. In cooler climates, maple trees store starch in their trunks and roots. Harvesting maple sap for syrup was not traditionally done by Newfoundlanders but it is becoming popular today.

HOW TO HARVEST

Tapping maple trees is an easy and fun way to start harvesting after a long Newfoundland winter. For the sap to begin flowing, the temperature needs to be below freezing at night and above freezing during the day. Usually on the Avalon maple syrup season is late March/early April. Ideally harvest from maples on your own property, or (with permission) on the property of friends or neighbours.

To tap maple trees, you will need basic supplies: a tap or spile; a hammer to insert the tap into the tree; a drill and drill bit slightly smaller than the tap or an old-fashioned wood auger (no batteries needed); and a bucket to catch the maple water coming from the tap. Use a bucket with a lid to keep hungry spring insects out.

EAT THE TREES (AND SHRUBS)

159

EAT THE TREES (AND SHRUBS)

Find a maple tree that is at least 10 inches in diameter. Trees that are 20-plus inches in diameter can be tapped multiple times. Use the drill or wood auger to drill a hole about 4 to 5 feet up from the base of the tree. Drill a 5-centimetre-deep hole on a slight incline so that the tap will point slightly downward. Remove any wood shavings and debris from the edge of the hole. Use a hammer and tap the spile gently into the tree. The sap should start to run immediately; have a bucket ready to hang under the taps. Check buckets frequently and empty them twice daily if necessary.

You can continue to harvest until the flowing maple water transitions from crystal clear to a cloudy liquid. At this point, remove the taps, sterilize them, and store them for the next maple season.

EAT THE TREES (AND SHRUBS)

Tapping will not hurt the tree, if it is done appropriately—but it is a good idea to give the maple a year off if the tree looks weak or unhealthy. Be sure to remove the spiles at the end of each season and the wounds will grow over within the year.

HOW TO USE

Use a large boiler to cook down maple water until it turns into a syrup. Keep the kitchen fan on constantly to remove the steam; cook outside on a propane burner if possible (but make sure there are no kids or animals around that could potentially knock over the boiling syrup—hot maple syrup can be very dangerous due to the heat of the natural sugar).

EAT THE TREES (AND SHRUBS)

EAT THE TREES (AND SHRUBS)

SPRUCE

White spruce, black spruce
Picea glauca, Picea mariana

May - June

WHAT IS IT?
White and black spruce are evergreen conifers commonly found across Newfoundland. The season's new growth or "tips" are often harvested for culinary use.

Both white and black spruce tips can be harvested, but white spruce tips have a stronger citrus taste and appear earlier in the spring. Black spruce needles are short, densely packed, and sharp; white spruce needles are upwardly arched and generally less densely packed than those of black spruce. In both species, the needles are arranged around the stem. Black spruce favours wet areas and are found along ponds, streams, and bogs. White spruce grows in drier areas.

To the untrained eye, spruce and fir look similar. To distinguish between the species, roll a needle between your fingers. Whereas the four-sided spruce needles roll easily, the flat fir needles do not. Both spruce and fir tips are edible, but spruce has the preferred flavour.

HOW TO HARVEST
Tender bright green spruce tips are a sure sign that summer is around the corner. Spruce tips have a strong citrus flavour and are rich in vitamin C.

Look for bright green spruce tips at the ends of tree branches. Snap them off with your fingers. Only collect a handful or two from each tree, being mindful not to disturb the tree's annual growth. Sometimes it helps to give the branch a hard slap or a shake to knock off the remaining husks.

Spruce tips are usually ready for collecting in May to June. Ideally, harvest when they are about 1 inch long until they become woody. Black spruce tips can often be harvested into July.

EAT THE TREES (AND SHRUBS)

EAT THE TREES (AND SHRUBS)

HOW TO USE

Spruce tips are a versatile ingredient in the kitchen. Use as a fresh herb: pull the needles apart and use to flavour any dish. Dehydrate spruce tips and use as a dried herb; they are a perfect substitute for rosemary.

Spruce tip oil: Remove any remaining husks from a handful of spruce tips. Wash, air-dry, and add to 1 cup of olive oil. Heat gently for 10 minutes, remove from the heat, cool, and strain. Refrigerate and use in a vinaigrette or as a dipping oil for bread (see beach green coleslaw recipe, page 103).

Add spruce tips to bread dough, your favourite shortbread cookies, or butter; infuse in oil or vinegar. Spruce tips can be pickled or candied.

Make spruce tip simple syrup (1:1:1 ratio of spruce tips, sugar, and water), jelly or pesto. Spruce tip salt and spruce tip sugar are both delicious and can be sprinkled on savoury and sweet dishes.

Fresh spruce tips are also used in brewing tea or making spruce beer.

EAT THE TREES (AND SHRUBS)

Spruce Tip Mortadella

Shaun Hussey, chef and co-owner, Chinched Restaurant and Deli, St. John's

5050 g pork shoulder
500 g pork fat, cubed (garnish) (scruncheons)
3 g cinnamon
3 g coriander
98 g sugar
82 g ground black pepper
1264 g ice

402 g spruce tips
3333 g fatback pork
8 g nutmeg
3 g cayenne
13 g cure #1
250 g skim milk powder
50 g fresh garlic

Dice the pork shoulder into cubes to fit your grinder.

Combine pork shoulder, pork fat scrunchions, and garlic in a bowl.

Grind 316 grams of ice with meat and fat on the largest size die in the grinder. Place mix in the refrigerator and chill to 4°C. Be sure to the mix does not get above 4°C. Repeat this step two more times, grinding each time with 316 grams of ice.

While the mix is chilling, weigh the rest of the ingredients.

Put meat mix and seasoning in a large mixing bowl and mix at medium speed until emulsified (about 3 minutes). Return to the fridge and prepare stuffer and casings.

Once the mix is loaded and packed (be sure to pack mix into the stuffer well to prevent air pockets) into the stuffer, begin piping the mortadella into the casing. Prick any visible air pockets and tie off tightly once full.

Allow the piped mortadella tubes to relax overnight in the refrigerator before cooking.

Prepare a simmering water bath to cook the mortadella tubes. Tighten the mortadella tubes with twine once more. Then wrap them tightly in multiple layers of plastic wrap.

Submerge the tubes in the simmering water bath. Insert a temperature probe, set to 155°C. Rotate the tubes every 30 minutes to prevent scorch marks.

EAT THE TREES (AND SHRUBS)

Shaun Hussey.

Once the tubes have reached 155°C internal temperature, remove and place in an ice bath for 1 to 2 hours. Remove from the ice bath and place on a sheet pan and cool in the refrigerator overnight.

Once cooled overnight, the mortadella is ready to slice and serve.

EAT THE TREES (AND SHRUBS)

SWEET GALE

Bog myrtle
Myrica gale

April - November

WHAT IS IT?

Sweet gale, a widespread shrub growing 1 to 2 metres tall, is frequently found on river- and pond banks and in bogs and other wet areas throughout Newfoundland. Matte green fragrant leaves are elongated, tapered at the base with a wider tip.

Plants flower early in the spring, before leaves appear. Male and female flowers (catkins) are on separate plants. Catkins are extremely aromatic and full of a waxy resin. Female flowers are tiny and red; male flowers are larger, about 1 centimetre long. Male flowers are green-yellow with brown scales when they bloom in early spring; they become dark brown as the season progresses.

HOW TO HARVEST

Harvest male catkins early in the spring. Leaves can be harvested throughout the growing season. Collect fruit in the fall.

HOW TO USE

Male flowers can be dried and used as a spice or for brewing and flavouring alcohol. Leaves can be collected and used as tea or treated like a bay leaf. The fruit is used as a spice, often added to soups or stews.

EAT THE TREES (AND SHRUBS)

EAT THE TREES (AND SHRUBS)

EAT THE TREES (AND SHRUBS)

TAMARACK

Eastern larch, juniper
Larix laricina

April - September

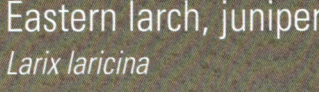    

WHAT IS IT?

Many in Newfoundland refer to these trees as "juniper"—tamarack products are often sold as juniper. Tamarack are in the pine family, but unlike most other conifers, their needles turn yellow in the fall and are lost during the winter. Needles are bluish green, relatively fine, soft, and flexible. Needles often grow in clusters, to 2 centimetres in length.

Trees are often found near spruce and fir, often in wetlands and beside water bodies.

HOW TO HARVEST

Tamarack leaves (needles) can be harvested from spring through summer, unlike spruce and fir tips. Pick bright green needles judiciously from trees.

Female cones are best harvested when they are vibrant purple in the spring and early summer—they turn brown later in the season, after shedding their seeds.

HOW TO USE

Use the needles fresh or dried as a herb. Make tamarack salt by first dehydrating the tamarack buds and then crushing with sea salt using a mortar and pestle.

The inner bark can be harvested, dried, pounded into a powder, and used as flour. Tamarack gum is sweet and can be chewed.

FORGOTTEN FRUITS AND GARDENS

Keep a sharp lookout as you hike or drive through resettled communities or pass abandoned homesteads—you may be surprised at the variety of plants that have escaped cultivation to stand the test of time. Apples, plums, damsons, rhubarb, and currants are found in unexpected abundance.

Some old homesteads may be on private property. If you think that this is the case, try to find the owners to ask permission before harvesting.

FORGOTTEN FRUIT AND GARDENS

FORGOTTEN FRUIT AND GARDENS

APPLE

Common apple, crabapple
Malus pumila

September - November

WHAT IS IT?

Most apple trees are hybrids, and a wide variety are found throughout Newfoundland along roadsides (where apple cores have been tossed) or near homesteads. It is common in Newfoundland to refer to all apples found in the wild as crabapples, but this is not actually the case. Crabapples are usually smaller and sharper tasting than common apples; many larger varieties of apples flourish and are sweet enough to eat straight from the tree. Take a bite.

Apple trees can reach to 10 metres tall and are usually as wide or wider than they are tall. The leaves are oval with toothed edges. Pink to white apple blossoms emerge in June; fruit ripens by early fall.

HOW TO HARVEST

Take care when climbing apple trees. Speaking from experience, mature trees often have weak or old branches that are apt to snap and result in a potentially serious fall. Late in the season, shake the branches and collect the apples that fall to the ground.

Collect apples that have dropped from the tree; check for insects or rot. These are especially suitable for making cider or vinegar.

HOW TO USE

Even notoriously tart crabapples have a place in the kitchen, in jams, jellies, and sauces.

Make apple cider, pies, applesauce, apple butter, or vinegar. Chop and add to baked goods. Use in jams and chutneys.

THE FORAGER'S DINNER

FORGOTTEN FRUIT AND GARDENS

Rosehip-Crabapple Jam

Elke Dettmer, Points East Guesthouse, Pouch Cove

Pick rosehips in the fall when they have turned bright red and are beginning to get soft, preferably after the first frost, which seems to improve their taste. Rosehips are particularly valued for their high vitamin C content. It is labour-intensive to separate the thin outside layer of fruit flesh from the mass of inner kernels. These kernels are known to itch—as children in Germany we would put some down each other's bare backs for a prank.

To process the rosehips, cut off the stems and dried flower parts, then either steam the cleaned fruit or boil them in a small amount of water, just enough to soften. Then comes the hard part. You can press the fruit through several layers of cheesecloth, leaving behind the mass of kernels, or use a contraption like the one I found in a flea market in Nova Scotia: a cone-shaped metal strainer with a fitted, hand-operated wooden pestle. Pressing a whole bucket of rosehips either through cheesecloth or a strainer yields a depressingly small amount of substance ready for jam, a good reason to add crabapples to the mix.

Crabapples complement the taste and the fine orange colour of the rosehips and add natural pectin. They tend to ripen at the same time as the rosehips and are much easier to prepare. I simply cut off the stems and the dried flower part, halve them, then boil briefly in a small amount of water until soft, and press them (easy) through cheesecloth or the strainer.

A good mix to make jam is one-half rosehip pulp, one-half crabapple pulp, but you can get away with one-third rosehip to two-thirds crabapple pulp. Boil the combined fruit with enough sugar to taste and to ensure its longevity (try two parts fruit to one part sugar to start), then process as other jam recipes.

FORGOTTEN FRUIT AND GARDENS

FORGOTTEN FRUIT AND GARDENS

BLACK ELDERBERRY

Sambucus sp.

August - October

WHAT IS IT?
Black, golden, and red elderberry trees are found in Newfoundland. Black and golden elderberry trees yield purple-black fruit; red elderberry fruit is red. Golden elderberry has golden leaves. Avoid harvesting from red elderberry trees, found primarily in western Newfoundland; the fruit is mildly toxic.

Elderberry trees grow to 5 metres or more tall. The leaves are compound, with up to seven lance-shaped leaflets. Elderberry flower buds are pink and open into large loose clusters of small white flowers.

Due to the short growing season in Newfoundland, elderberry fruit rarely have time to ripen.

HOW TO HARVEST
Snip flowers in full bloom where the stem meets the tree. During an especially warm summer, you may be lucky enough to find ripe black fruit.

HOW TO USE
Infuse elderberry flowers to make syrup, cordial, flavoured gin, or tea. Use in making ice cream and baking.

The fruit should be cooked before consuming and can be made into jams, sauces, or syrups.

FORGOTTEN FRUIT AND GARDENS

CURRANTS

Ribes spp.

July - August

WHAT IS IT?
Black, red, and (less common) white currants are upright to sprawling shrubs to 1.5 metres high. Currant canes bear three- to five-lobed leaves, 3 to 8 centimetres in diameter. Small pink-white flowers are followed by bunches of round glossy fruit.

Currants grow well in many habitats, including damp soil, and open, rocky areas. Gooseberries are in the same family and are found in similar habitats. Look for oval green to purple fruit.

HOW TO HARVEST
Currants and gooseberries ripen through August and September. Watch for thorns while picking gooseberries.

HOW TO USE
Raw black, red, and white currants are tart and are generally processed before eating; red and white currants are better raw than black currants. High in pectin, currants are ideal for jams and jellies. Combine with other seasonal berries or fruit in pies and other baked goods.

Black currants are particularly suited to cordials, syrups, or alcohol infusions.

FORGOTTEN FRUIT AND GARDENS

FORGOTTEN FRUIT

Damson Plum Chutney

Karen Willoughby, Handmade by Hand

Serve this chutney with fishcakes, spread on handmade bread, or just about any dish.

2 lbs damson plums, cleaned, pitted, and roughly chopped
1 large onion, diced
Handful garlic cloves, smashed and finely diced
Canola oil
Maple syrup
2–3 sprigs thyme
¼ cup yellow mustard seeds
¼ cup brown mustard seeds
1 cup apple cider vinegar
2 cups water
1 cup sugar
Salt
Cracked black pepper to taste
Ground cinnamon, cumin, or coriander to taste

On medium heat, pour canola oil into a large saucepan—just enough to cover the bottom when you swirl it around.
    Toast the mustard seeds in the oil until just fragrant.
    Add the onions and garlic and sweat them out with the fresh thyme until the onions are translucent.
    Add the damsons and all other ingredients. Turn the heat to low and allow the mixture to simmer until it has thickened and can coat the back of a spoon.
    Salt, pepper, and spices are to taste; add and adjust accordingly.
    Let cool to room temperature. Bottle the chutney to preserve or refrigerate.

FORGOTTEN FRUIT AND GARDENS

FORGOTTEN FRUIT AND GARDENS

FORSYTHIA

Easter tree
Forsythia sp.

 May - June

WHAT IS IT?
Forsythia trees burst into bright yellow flowers in spring, before any leaves appear. The four-lobed flowers close into a distinctive pendant shape in the rain, protecting the reproductive parts. Forsythia are usually 1 to 3 metres tall, with rough grey-brown bark and a tangle of thin branches. Oval leaves are opposite, abundant, and about 5 centimetres long.

HOW TO HARVEST
Pick flowers when in full bloom, usually in May.

HOW TO USE
Add flowers to salads or cocktails or use as a garnish.

Harvest the branches in the winter and place in water in a south-facing window. This will force the flowers to emerge early for late winter or early spring colour.

FORGOTTEN FRUIT AND GARDENS

FORGOTTEN FRUIT AND GARDENS

LILAC

Syringa vulgaris

WHAT IS IT?

Lilac is a tall, gangly shrub with multiple stems and suckers. Its light green leaves are up to 12 centimetres long, oval, and opposite.

The aromatic purple, pink, or white flowers bloom in dense elongated clusters in late spring and early summer. Flowers are tubelike, with four lobes.

HOW TO HARVEST

Lilac flowers grow at the tips of branches. Snap flower clusters off by hand or use pruners. The flowers do not last long, so harvest when you see them.

HOW TO USE IT

Steep lilac flowers in cream to make custard, ice cream, whipped cream, or other desserts.

Sprinkle flowers on salad or desserts for a garnish.

To make a lilac simple syrup, simmer flowers gently with sugar and water (a ratio of 1:1:1), leave to steep for a few hours, and strain. Use in cocktails, cordials, or elixirs.

FORGOTTEN FRUIT AND GARDENS

Lilac + Honey Pie

Stephanie Mackenzie, Woodstock Public House

Lilac sugar
1 cup sugar
2 cups lilac flowers (no stems)

Mix together a couple of days before making the pie.

Pie filling
½ cup unsalted butter, melted and cooled
¾ cup lilac sugar
1 tbsp cornmeal
½ tsp kosher salt
1 tsp vanilla paste
¾ cup honey
½ cup heavy cream
3 large eggs
2 tsp white vinegar
½ cup lilac flowers (no stems)

Pie crust, prebaked

Use your favourite pie crust recipe. Prebake the crust and let cool.
    In a medium bowl, stir together the melted butter, lilac sugar, cornmeal, and vanilla paste. Stir in the honey and the eggs, one at a time. Stir in the heavy cream and vinegar. Gently mix in the lilac flowers.
    Preheat oven to 350°C.
    Pour the filling into the cooled pie crust. Bake (with no fan) for about 40 to 45 minutes, rotating halfway through. The pie is done when the edges are set and puffed and the centre looks set like gelatin.

FORGOTTEN FRUIT AND GARDENS

FORGOTTEN FRUIT AND GARDENS

PLUM

Prunus sp.

WHAT IS IT?
Several varieties of plums grow "wild" in Newfoundland, most transported to the province by European settlers. Plum trees tend to be tall (6 to 10 metres) and skinny—not appropriate for climbing—with dark grey bark and thorns. Five-petalled white flowers bloom in late spring.

The fruit most commonly has blue to purple skin and soft orange-gold flesh surrounding a large pit. Greengage plums are sweet and green-gold in colour. Plums tend to be slightly larger and more evenly round than damsons.

HOW TO HARVEST
Harvest plums in the fall, after a frost.

HOW TO USE
Plums are sweeter than damsons and can be enjoyed raw.
Make jam, jelly, sauce, tarts, and other baked goods.

FORGOTTEN FRUIT AND GARDENS

FORGOTTEN FRUIT AND GARDENS

RHUBARB

Rheum rhabarbarum

May - August

WHAT IS IT?
Rhubarb is one of the first plants to pop up in the spring—pink-red crowns can be seen poking through the ground as the snow recedes in April or early May.

Rhubarb stalks are thick (to 2 centimetres in diameter) and green to pink-red. Each stalk bears a single large, thick triangular leaf.

HOW TO HARVEST
Cut rhubarb stalks regularly throughout the summer; do not let the plants flower and you'll have weeks or months of harvest. Discard the leaves around the base of the plant and use as compost.

HOW TO USE
Rhubarb is tangy and suited to a range of condiments (chutney, BBQ sauce, pickles) and jam. Combine with sweeter fruit such as apples, strawberries, or blueberries, for jams, pies, and other desserts.

Chop stalks and add to cakes, muffins, and other baked goods. Simmer rhubarb in water, then strain. Use the juice for rhubarb lemonade, cocktails, and more.

Leaves are high in oxalic acid and should not be consumed.

FORGOTTEN FRUIT AND GARDENS

FORGOTTEN FRUIT AND GARDENS

Rhubarb-Crow-Chuckley Chutney

Chef Amy Anthony

This is great on a moose burger, salmon, or baked brie.

1 lb rhubarb, chopped
2 local sweet red onions, small dice
1 cup currants, soaked in port overnight
1 cup chuckley pears
2 cups crowberries
2 cups cider vinegar
3 tbsp brown mustard seed
3 tbsp Newfoundland Salt Company Smoked Juniper Salt
3 cloves garlic, minced
1 thumb-sized piece of fresh ginger, minced
2 tsp cinnamon
¼ tsp paprika
¼ tsp cardamom
Pinch of cloves
¼ tsp chili flakes

Heave it all into a pot, bring to a boil, and simmer 30 minutes until thickened.
    Bottle to preserve or keep in the refrigerator.

FORGOTTEN FRUIT AND GARDENS

Amy Anthony.

FORGOTTEN FRUIT AND GARDENS

FORGOTTEN FRUIT AND GARDENS

WILD HOPS

Humulus lupulus

WHAT IS IT?
Hops, a cousin to the cannabis plant, was introduced to the island of Newfoundland by early European settlers, who used the flowers in their breadmaking. This perennial vine has broad, heart-shaped opposite leaves and a prickly stalk. Plants can grow to 15 metres tall and are often found along the edges of overgrown fields or entangled with old pin cherry stands and forgotten apple trees.

Male and female flowers are found on the same plants; "hops" generally refers to the greenish seed cones (female flowers).

HOW TO HARVEST
Harvest the tender shoots in late May/early June by snapping them off under the first pair of opposite leaves, or at the point the stalk becomes fibrous and difficult to snap. The window for harvesting shoots is quite short, so check patches frequently and early. Leaves can be picked a little longer into the season, until they become tough.

Pick flower buds when they have developed into a 1- to 2-centimetre-long cone, in late August until mid-September.

HOW TO USE
Sauté, boil, or serve shoots raw with a vinaigrette; they can also be battered and fried or deep-fried.

Use the young leaves in a salad or steam like spinach.

Use flowers to make bitters for cocktails or in beer-making.

FORGOTTEN FRUIT AND GARDENS

SHAWN DAWSON

Pickled Wild Hops Shoots

Shawn Dawson

I like to pickle hops shoots in an IPA brine.

- 4 cups fresh wild hops shoots
- 1 cup apple cider vinegar
- 1 cup Quidi Vidi Calm Tom Double IPA
- ½ cup water
- 4 tbsp brown sugar
- 2 tbsp salt
- ½ tsp chili flakes
- 1 tbsp mustard seed
- 1 tbsp juniper berries
- 4 cloves garlic, sliced thin

Combine all ingredients except the shoots in a large saucepan. Simmer the brine until the sugar dissolves. Add the shoots and continue to simmer for 3 to 4 minutes. Pack into sterilized jars, process, and store.

BERRIES

When many people think of foraging in Newfoundland, berries are the first foods that come to mind. Rightfully so: we have some of the most beautiful, varied, and productive berry grounds in the world.

Berry picking has a long tradition in this province, as a family activity and a source of income. To ensure that this continues, keep a few guidelines in mind. Do not over-pick berry patches or use berry rakes, which are destructive to bushes. Avoid using ATVs on bogs, marshes, and other berry grounds: not only do ATVs damage berry bushes and shrubs, but they are also a source of pollution for vulnerable wetlands.

BERRIES

BAKEAPPLE

Cloudberry
Rubus chamaemorus

July - August

WHAT IS IT?
Bakeapples are a Newfoundland treasure—competition for berries and secrecy around berry patches can be fierce. Look for these low-growing berries (to 15 centimetres) in marshes, bogs, and other windswept, open areas. Bakeapples are most prolific close to the coastline.

Bakeapple plants have up to five dark green, lobed, wrinkled leaves. A single white-petalled flower per plant is followed by a 1.5-centimetre-diameter orange-red berry.

HOW TO HARVEST
Because each bakeapple plant produces just one berry, harvesting is a potentially back-breaking and time-consuming task. They are usually ready for picking in early August; wait until they are fully ripe (yellow-orange and soft) to harvest.

Resist the urge to collect bakeapples when they are still hard and unripe. This can damage the plant and yields a less flavoursome berry.

HOW TO USE
Make bakeapple jam, sauce, cheesecakes, and other desserts. Serve bakeapple jam with cream.

BERRIES

Banks & Shores

Barrens

Clearings

Disturbed Areas

Forest

Wetlands

BERRIES

Warm Bakeapple Scruncheon Vinaigrette
with Lemon Pepper Cod and Vegetable Succotash

Chef Mark McCrowe

Rubus chamaemorus, also known as cloudberry for its cumulus cloudlike characteristics, or Nordic berry for its Viking intuitions to thrive in a cold northern climate. I always knew them as bakeapples growing up in Newfoundland and spending time in Long Harbour with my Nan, who was always at the ready to go for a pick when the time of year was right.

My favourite memory is a simple one: Freshly baked bread with a little butter and a thick slathering of bakeapple jam. Even as a kid I knew bakeapples were an acquired taste, something truly Newfoundland and sour as the bogs they came from. But realizing that you can balance something sour like the wild berries with sweet was a big moment for me as a kid—an aha! food moment. That balance of sour and sweet fascinates me to this day, and this bakeapple scruncheon vinaigrette plays with this idea. It's all about the balance of the tart berries, the sweetness of the honey, and the saltiness of the salt pork, all tied together with a burst of freshly squeezed lemon juice and fresh basil.

It makes sense to me to pair this vinaigrette with delicate cod simply roasted with lemon zest, cracked pepper, and a celebration of local seasonal vegetables cooked together with love in an epic succotash of the garden.

BERRIES

THE FORAGER'S DINNER

BERRIES

Bakeapple scruncheon vinaigrette
1 cup salt pork scruncheons, diced
1 cup bakeapples
½ cup honey
¼ cup lemon juice
2 tbsp extra-virgin olive oil
Fresh cracked pepper
2 tbsp basil chiffonade

Render the pork scruncheons until golden brown and crispy in a small saucepan. Strain off the excess fat and reserve. In a bowl, whisk together the scruncheons with the remaining ingredients. Slowly drizzle in the reserved pork fat to emulsify the vinaigrette. Check the seasoning and adjust to taste. Serve warm, but do not boil or the sauce will split.

Lemon pepper cod
4 6-oz fillets of fresh cod
Sea salt
Coarsely ground black pepper
Zest of two lemons

Place the cod fillets on a baking sheet lined with parchment paper. Season evenly and roast at 400°F for about 10 minutes or until the cod is just cooked through.

Local vegetable succotash
I'm going to leave this up to you. It's a one-pan wonder of diced sautéed vegetables—just make sure to start with vegetables with longer cooking times, like potatoes or squash, adding in others as you go. I use butter, add a touch of honey, and finish with a fresh herb like cilantro, basil, parsley, or chives. It's the perfect way to use the best of the season.

I serve this family-style with a mountain of succotash on a large platter. Top with the cod portions and then drizzle the warm bakeapple vinaigrette over the top. Garnish the dish with a few extra bakeapples, baby basil leaves, and some extra-crispy scruncheons. Enjoy!

BERRIES

Mark McCrowe.

BERRIES
BLACKBERRY

Rubus canadensis

August - September

WHAT IS IT?

Blackberries are bramble-type berries that grow on a thick tangle of thorny bushes about 1 metre high. Its compound leaves have usually five but up to seven leaflets and are covered in stiff, prickly hairs. The white flowers have five petals. The shiny berries are raspberry-like in shape and change from red to a deep purple-black as they ripen.

Blackberry bushes grow in clearings and disturbed areas, including roadsides, cutovers, and burn sites.

HOW TO HARVEST

Blackberries on a single bush ripen at different times over several weeks, usually late August into September. Selectively harvest ripe berries; you may need to make multiple visits to a patch.

HOW TO USE

Snack on raw blackberries raw or use in a salad. Make jam or pies or add to baked goods. Mix into a vinaigrette.

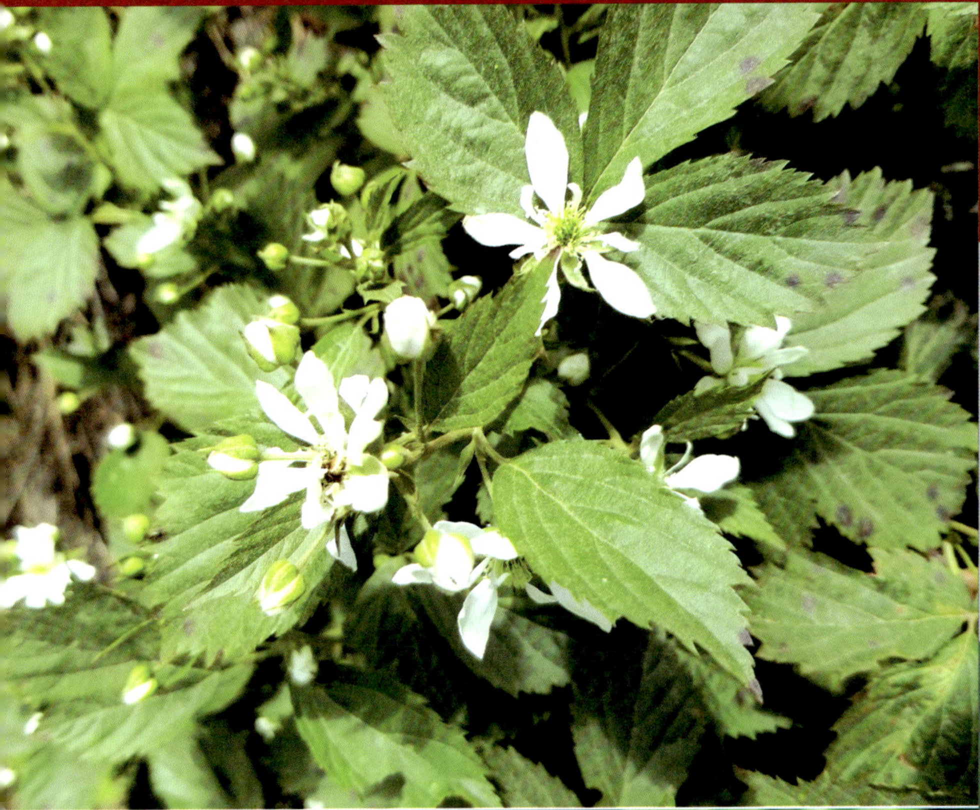

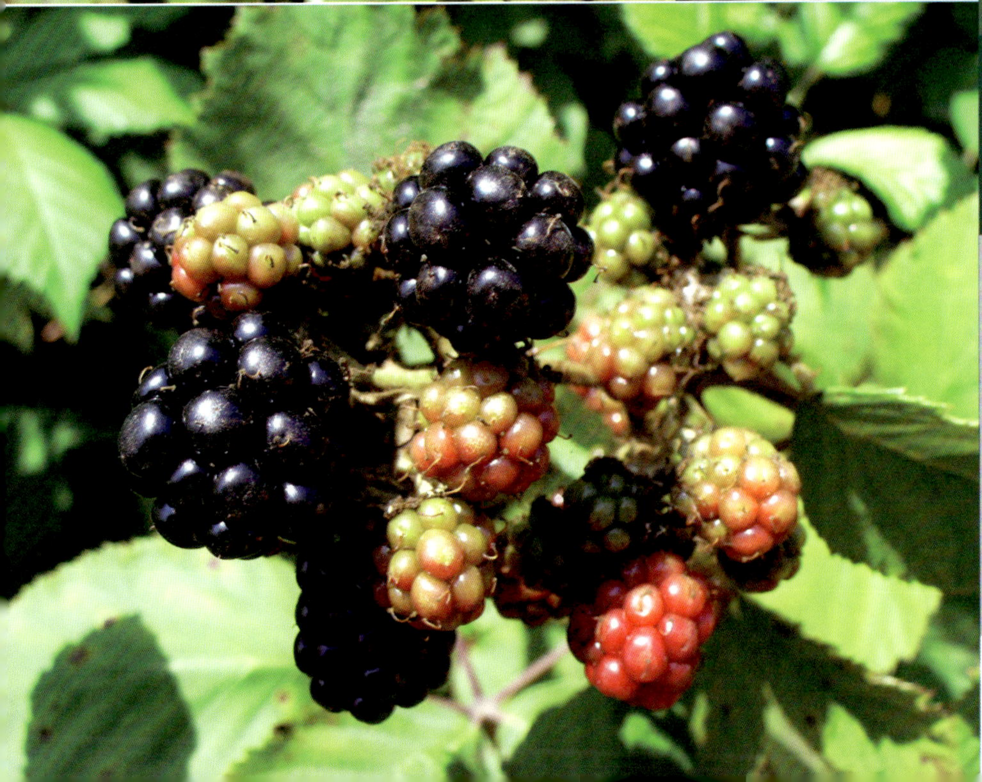

Banks & Shores
Barrens
Clearings
Disturbed Areas
Forest
Wetlands

BERRIES

BERRIES

BLUEBERRY

Vaccinium angustifolium

August - September

WHAT IS IT?
Next to codfish, blueberries are one of Newfoundland's finest assets; many in this province proudly proclaim that we have the best-tasting, most nutrient-dense blueberries in the world. In a good season, blueberries are bountiful in clearings, disturbed areas, and barrens and along coastlines.

Found in patches, blueberry shrubs grow to 30 centimetres tall or more. Its narrow oval-shaped leaves are shiny green and turn a deep red in the fall. White or pale pink bell-shaped flowers are followed by round berries growing in bunches.

Several species of blueberry are found in Newfoundland and vary in bush height and leaf shape. All berries are edible.

HOW TO HARVEST
Pick berries by hand when ripe (do not use a berry rake). Try not to over-harvest; leave some for propagation and for the birds.

HOW TO USE
Eat blueberries raw by the handful or toss on yogurt, cereal, or salads.

Blueberries make exceptional jam and pies. Add to muffins and other baked goods. Try in a chutney or blueberry-jalapeno hot sauce.

Blueberry steamed pudding is part of the traditional Newfoundland Sunday dinner.

BERRIES

BUNCHBERRY

Crackerjacks, crackerberry
Cornus canadensis

WHAT IS IT?
Bunchberry plants grow in large patches on the forest floor, usually along trails and under a canopy of trees. The plants are 10 to 15 centimetres tall with four to six shiny, green, deeply veined leaves. The four-petalled white flowers have yellow centres and yield bunches of showy red-orange berries.

Bunchberries have a seed that cracks or pops when bitten, giving this plant its other common name.

HOW TO HARVEST
Berries ripen in August.

HOW TO USE
Bunchberries are tasteless on their own but can be added to other red berry jams as a natural source of pectin.

Because of their high water content, bunchberries are a bland but useful hiking snack.

BERRIES

215

BERRIES

BERRIES

CHOKEBERRY

Aronia berry
Photinia floribunda, Photinia melanocarpa

August - September

WHAT IS IT?
Chokeberries are found in wetlands and along rivers, streams, and ponds. These shrubs are 1 to 1.5 metres tall; leathery oval-shaped green leaves have finely toothed edges and a blunt toothed tip.

The five-petalled white flowers are in clusters and often have pink stamens. Purple to deep black berries are produced in late August through September.

HOW TO HARVEST
Harvest berries when they are nearly black.

HOW TO USE
Chokeberries are quite astringent when eaten raw. Use to make wine, jam, or jelly.

BERRIES

BERRIES

CHOKECHERRY

Prunus virginiana

August - September

WHAT IS IT?
Chokecherry trees grow to 6 metres but are most often about half that height. These trees have grey bark and are suckering and often found in large stands. The dark green oval toothed leaves have pale undersides; leaves turn yellow in the fall. Downward-bending chains of clustered white flowers are followed by bunches of red to purple berries.

Chokecherry trees are less common than pin cherries, the other Newfoundland wild cherry.

HOW TO HARVEST
Chokecherries grow in bunches and are relatively easy to pick in quantity. Wait until the fruit is dark purple before harvesting.

HOW TO USE
As the name suggests, and much like chokeberries, chokecherries are astringent when eaten raw. Use to make wine, jam, or jelly. Chokecherries have a seed which must be strained out after cooking.

BERRIES

BERRIES

CHUCKLEY PEAR

Saskatoon berry, serviceberry, shadblow, juneberry, chuckleberry *Amelanchier* sp.

July - August

WHAT IS IT?

Chuckley pear is a short tree, usually between 1 and 3 metres in height, but can reach 8 metres in certain locations. Its oval leaves have toothed edges. Its white five-petalled flowers are among the first spring blooms. Chuckley pear fruit are round to oblong and change colour from pink-red to purple to near black as they ripen.

Six species of chuckley pear are found in Newfoundland; all chuckley pear trees bear edible fruit. Trees grow along the edges of old trails, in forests and disturbed areas, and on riverbanks.

HOW TO HARVEST

Harvest chuckley pears when they are deep purple to black and slightly soft to the touch. Do not wait too long—ripe chuckley pears are a favourite of birds.

Collect aromatic spring buds; they taste and smell like marzipan.

HOW TO USE

Eat chuckley pears raw or use to make wine, pies, tarts, jam, or chutney.

Use spring buds to infuse alcohol.

BERRIES

CRANBERRY

Vaccinium macrocarpon,
Vaccinium oxycocus (marshberry)

September - April

WHAT IS IT?

Cranberry and its close relative marshberry are found in wetlands and on barrens and cliffsides, especially near the ocean. Both are low-lying plants with threadlike creeping stems and oblong evergreen leaves that tend to roll under; marshberry leaves tend to be wider at the base. Cranberry leaves turn red-purple in the fall.

Ripe cranberries are pink-red spheres; marshberries are oval and generally slightly smaller than cranberries.

HOW TO HARVEST

Both berries ripen in late fall and taste best after a frost. Cranberries, in particular, can be harvested through the winter and even into the spring.

HOW TO USE

Cranberries and marshberries have a similar tart taste. Use interchangeably to make jam, jelly, sauce, and other desserts.

Cranberry catsup is delicious on moose burgers, homemade fries, or chicken. To make: dry-fry onions and mustard seeds in a small saucepan until the mustard seeds start to pop. Add 1 cup cranberries and 1 cup brown sugar; simmer over medium heat until the cranberries soften. Add ½ cup apple cider vinegar and a pinch of cinnamon. Store in the refrigerator or bottle to preserve.

BERRIES

223

BERRIES

CREEPING SNOWBERRY

Tea berries, magna-tea berry, maidenhair berry, capillaire *Gaultheria hispidula*

August - September

WHAT IS IT?

Creeping snowberries grow on slim stems that creep along the forest floor. Look for them under trees and along pathways.

The shiny green oval leaves are about 1 centimetre long. Its oval-shaped small white fruit ripen in August. The entire plant, including the fruit, is covered with tiny, stiff, rust-coloured hairs.

HOW TO HARVEST

The fruit can be tricky to harvest as they grow underneath the leaves. Brush your hand across the top of a patch of snowberry vines to expose the berries—you may be surprised how plentiful they are.

HOW TO USE

Creeping snowberry fruit and leaves have a delicate wintergreen flavour. Add snowberries to any berry dishes or jams. If you have the patience to pick enough snowberries, use to infuse alcohol.

Use leaves and stems for tea or to flavour a moose roast.

BERRIES

225

BERRIES

CROWBERRY

Moss berry, blackberry
Empetrum nigrum

WHAT IS IT?
Look for crowberries in the same places you find blueberries, especially on coastal barrens and open heaths. Crowberries grow in dense mats up to 15 centimetres thick. At first glance, plants resemble moss, with a tight tangle of stems covered in densely crowded rod-shaped leaves. Small reddish flowers appear in early spring and are followed by black, round berries by late July.

Watch for purple paintlike splatters of bird poop on rocks as you hike along the coasts—seagulls and other shorebirds also feast on crowberries.

HOW TO HARVEST
Pick crowberries when they are black and firm.

HOW TO USE
Crowberries are fairly bland but are juicy and sweeten as they ripen. Make crowberry pudding, jam, chutney, or ice cream. Combine with apples in a pie filling.

BERRIES

227

BERRIES

DEWBERRY

Hairy plumboy, ground raspberry
Rubus pubescens

July - August

WHAT IS IT?
Dewberry plants are short (15 to 20 centimetres), creeping perennial plants. They grow in clearings and cut-overs, grassy areas at forest edges, and along old trails. Its shiny leaves are diamond-shaped with toothed edges. The flowers are white to pale pink. Dewberry fruit are red- to deep red-black and are shaped like raspberries.

Dewberries are a rare treat to find in abundance; when you do find a productive patch, you will never forget it.

HOW TO HARVEST
Dewberries ripen throughout a two- to three-week period, starting in mid-July.

HOW TO USE
Dewberry jam is my all-time favourite jam. Add dewberries to any baked goods or pie. Use to make wine.

BERRIES

BERRIES

BERRIES

DOGBERRY

American mountain ash, European mountain ash, showy mountain ash, rowanberry *Sorbus* spp.

WHAT IS IT?

According to Newfoundland folklore, an autumnal abundance of dogberry fruit forecasts a harsh winter ahead—or a harsh winter gone by, depending on the speaker.

Several species of dogberry grow in Newfoundland; all bear distinctive bunches of edible bright red-orange fruit. These deciduous trees grow to 3 metres tall. The compound leaves have up to 17 evenly spaced, lance-shaped opposite leaflets. White flowers in a dense, flat-topped cluster bloom in late June to July. The fruit have a starlike tip, left by the remains of the flower.

Dogberry trees are found in varied locations: woodlands, rocky terrain, seaside cliffs, barrens, burn sites and other disturbed areas and on the edges of clearings.

HOW TO HARVEST

The fruit are usually ready to harvest in early fall; wait for the colour to deepen to red-orange and the berries to soften slightly. The large clusters make it relatively easy to collect large amounts. Dogberries are a favourite of birds, so be sure to leave some behind.

HOW TO USE

Dogberry fruit are dry and unpalatable but are commonly used to make wine. Combine dogberries and crabapples (two fruit that are not known for having a pleasant taste) to make surprisingly delicioius jellies, pies, and jams.

BERRIES

BERRIES

HIGH-BUSH CRANBERRY

Viburnum opulus

September - March

WHAT IS IT?
Despite its name, high-bush cranberry is more closely related to squashberry than the low-lying cranberry. High-bush cranberry shrubs have grey bark and are usually about waist height but can grow to 3 metres tall. The paired leaves (6 to 10 centimetres long) have three pointed lobes and turn red in the autumn.

Clusters of white flowers appear at the ends of branches in late July. Shiny bright red fruit follow in late summer and remain on the branches into the winter after the leaves have fallen—if the birds don't feast on them first.

HOW TO HARVEST
Pick ripe berries in September and into the winter.

HOW TO USE
High-bush cranberries are sweeter than ground cranberries, but as they have a seed in the middle, they are better suited to jelly and sauces than jam.

Eat fresh; they are a delightful snack on a winter snowshoeing trip.

BERRIES
NORTHERN WILD RAISIN

Viburnum nudum var. *cassinoides*

September - October

WHAT IS IT?
A deciduous shrub growing to 3 metres tall, northern wild raisin is found in damp areas and clearings, next to ponds, on riverbanks, and along the treeline. Its elongated leaves are opposite and have few, if any, teeth along the edges. The leaves are copper-coloured in the spring but become shiny green in summer and bright red in autumn.

Clusters of white flowers emerge in the spring; clusters of oval fruit ripen to near black in late summer into the fall. The fruit (5 to 12 millimetres in diameter) have a large seed. Look for long silver brown buds in the winter.

HOW TO HARVEST
Fruit ripen gradually and at different rates; one cluster may have ripening white and pink, as well as ripe purple-black, fruit. Shrivelled fruit are also tasty and worth harvesting.

HOW TO USE
Northern wild raisin has a raisin-prune flavour. The large seed must be removed after cooking. Make jelly, juice, or wine.

Eat fruit raw when ripe or, better, when they have dried and shrivelled.

BERRIES

BERRIES

PARTRIDGEBERRY

Lingonberry, red berry, mountain cranberry, fox berry   *Vaccinium vitis-idaea*

WHAT IS IT?

Perhaps Newfoundland's favourite red berry, partridgeberries are found growing in mats on barrens and other windswept and rocky open areas, particularly near the ocean. Its glossy green oval leaves have a distinct central crease. The deep red round fruit are smaller (1 centimetre in diameter) than cranberries.

Partridgeberries are host to the lingonberry fruitworm, the larvae of the moth *Grapholita libertina*. Fruitworms leave the berries in late summer, after frost.

HOW TO HARVEST

Harvest partridgeberries after the first frost for the best flavour and to avoid picking berries with fruitworm inside.

HOW TO USE

Add these tart red berries to any baked goods. Make jam, pies, sauces, or wine.

BERRIES

Partridgeberry Cake

Kayla O'Brien, chef and owner, Fork Restaurant, Mobile

2 cups brown sugar
1½ cups oil
4 eggs
1 tsp vanilla
½ can (20 oz) crushed pineapple
2 grated apples
2 cups partridgeberries
2 cups all-purpose flour
¾ tbsp baking soda
¼ tsp salt
1 tsp cinnamon

Icing
½ cup salted butter, softened
8 oz cream cheese, softened
1 tsp vanilla extract
4 cups icing sugar

Combine the brown sugar and oil. Add the eggs, vanilla, pineapple, and apples. In a separate bowl, combine the flour, soda, salt, and cinnamon.
 Add the dry ingredients to the wet and mix. Add the partridgeberries and mix gently. Pour the batter into a 16 by 21-inch baking sheet or two 13 by 9-inch pans.
 Bake at 350°F for approximately 25 minutes, or until a toothpick comes out clean. Let cool and then ice.

Icing: combine all ingredients using an electric mixer. Whip at high speed until light and fluffy. Enjoy!

BERRIES

BERRIES

PIN CHERRY

Prunus pensylvanica

August - September

WHAT IS IT?
Pin cherry is common and widespread across the province on hillsides, in clearings and disturbed areas, and along the edges of ponds. Trees grow to 8 metres, generally taller than chokecherry trees. The bark is shiny grey. Its lance-shaped downward-hanging leaves are folded inward slightly along the centre rib. The leaves turn orange-red in autumn.

Its five-petalled white flowers bloom in June and July, then become long-stalked iridescent red fruit.

Pin cherry is susceptible to black knot fungus, which also infects plum, damson, and ornamental cherry trees in the province. Fruit are still edible from a tree with black knot.

HOW TO HARVEST
Pick fruit as they ripen in August and early September. Don't wait too long; birds are quick to strip the trees of fruit.

HOW TO USE
Pin cherries have a large seed that needs to be strained out. Use the pulp or juice to make jelly, wine, or soda.

BERRIES

Banks & Shores

Barrens

Clearings

Disturbed Areas

Forest

Wetlands

241

BERRIES

BERRIES

RASPBERRY

Rubus idaeus

August

WHAT IS IT?
Wild red raspberries grow in thickets in recently disturbed areas, including logged-over sites, burn sites, gravel pits, and roadsides. Its compound leaves have three to seven pointed leaflets, hairless upper surfaces, and hairy undersides. The thorny canes grow to 1 metre tall.

These canes live two years and produce red fruit (1 to 2 centimetres in diameter) in their second year. The fruit ripens in August.

HOW TO HARVEST
Raspberries are perfectly ripe when they are deep red, soft, and fall off the bush as you harvest.

HOW TO USE
Process or freeze raspberries immediately after harvesting; they will go mouldy within a day or two.

Eat these prized berries raw or make jam, pies, cheesecakes, and other desserts and baked goods.

Make tea from dried or fresh leaves.

BERRIES

Kevin Massey.

Campfire-Cooked Raspberry Upside-Down Cake

Kevin Massey, The Old Dublin Bakery, St. John's

2 cups wild Newfoundland raspberries
1 cup white sugar
1 cup plus 2 tablespoons salted butter, not refrigerated
4 eggs
1½ cups flour
Pinch salt

Light the campfire and set up an area of hot coals or stones, ready for your pan. If no fire is possible, use your own stove or a camp stove.

Heat an 8-inch cast iron pan to medium heat.

In a bowl, soften 1 cup of the butter with the sugar and mix with a wooden spoon until soft, creamy, and light.

Crack the eggs and mix lightly. Add the eggs to the butter mixture one at a time, mixing with the wooden spoon until fully incorporated.

Stir the flour into the mixture in three or four increments, mixing gently each time, just until mixed. When all the flour has been incorporated, sprinkle with a little salt. Set aside.

In the warm cast iron pan, melt 2 tablespoons butter and gently coat the entire pan with it using a brush or paper towel. Remove the pan from the heat, sprinkle the raspberries in evenly and spread the cake batter on top of the raspberries evenly and smoothly. Cover the pan tightly with a layer of parchment paper and a layer of tinfoil, return the pan to the hot coals or medium burner, and cook as evenly as possible for 20 to 25 minutes. Gently lift a corner to check on the pan as needed.

When the cake is golden brown and springs back when gently pressed, it is ready. It may appear moist with the raspberries underneath.

Best served warm with strong black tea at your favourite campsite.

BERRIES

BERRIES

ROSE

Shining rose, Virginia rose, shrub roses
Rosa nitida, Rosa virginiana, Rosa spp.

July - December

WHAT IS IT?

Wild roses, as well as larger-bloomed roses that have escaped cultivation, are found across the province along roadsides and trails, in damp thickets and clearings, and on rocky slopes and barrens. Wild roses (shining rose and Virginia rose) are shorter in stature (1 to 2 metres) than "wild" escapes (3 metres or more). The flowers range from small five-petalled light pink blooms to large double flowers. The first flowers emerge in July; the shrubs may continue flowering into September.

Flowers are followed by rosehips: red tomato-like fruit with a dried crown.

HOW TO HARVEST

Pick flowers in the morning, when they are at their most fragrant. Never strip a rose shrub of all its flowers.

Rosehips taste best after the first frost. They can be picked through the fall and into the winter.

HOW TO USE

Use rose petals for flavouring desserts or cocktails. Candy petals using egg white and sugar to use as a garnish. Make rosewater or a simple syrup. Dry petals for year-round use.

Make rosehip jam, jelly, or chutney.

BERRIES

Rose + Rhubarb Cocktail
Jessica Gibson, Toslow, St. John's

For the syrup
4 cups rhubarb, roughly chopped
1 cup + 2 tbsp sugar
2 cups water
1 cup freshly picked wild rose petals
Juice of ½ lemon

For the cocktail (serves 2)
4 oz gin
1 oz St. Germaine elderflower liqueur
2 oz freshly squeezed lemon juice
1 ½ oz rhubarb-rose syrup
Ice

Make the syrup (best done a day or two in advance):
Let the chopped rhubarb macerate in 2 tablespoons sugar for at least 30 minutes. Place the rhubarb and the juices that were released during the maceration in a heavy-bottomed saucepan with the water and rose petals. Bring to a boil.

Add 1 cup of sugar and bring to a boil again, allowing the sugar to dissolve. Remember to stir throughout this process so that your ingredients don't burn! Add the juice of half a small lemon, turn off the heat, and cover. Let the mixture sit for a few hours or overnight to allow the flavours to develop.

When the syrup taste is to your liking, strain the rhubarb and rose petal pulp through a mesh sieve. Double strain if possible. This process may take a half hour to an hour, so feel free to just let it drip into a deep bowl or jar.

Pour the syrup into a clean jar with a lid and refrigerate. The syrup should last 1 to 2 weeks in the refrigerator.

BERRIES

Make the cocktail
Pack a cocktail shaker about three-quarters full of ice. Fill two glasses with ice. Pour the gin, elderflower liqueur, lemon juice, and rhubarb-rose syrup into the ice-filled shaker. Cap and shake for about 30 seconds so that the shaker is cold to the touch and the liquid inside is aerated.

Pour into the glasses over ice, top with 3 oz of soda water each (optional), garnish with a slice of lemon and a rose petal, and enjoy!

BERRIES
SKUNK CURRANT

Ribes glanulosum

July - August

WHAT IS IT?
Skunk currants are one of the first woodland shrubs to leaf out in the spring. These shrubs are usually about 1 metre in height, though occasionally up to 2 metres. Its five-lobed leaves have toothed edges, similar to cultivated currant leaves. White to pink five-petalled flowers grow in upright clusters; the flower stalks are sticky. The fruit are small (0.5 to 1 centimetre in diameter), brilliant shiny red, and covered in fine hairs.

Skunk currant shrubs often grow among Labrador tea and other shrubs in the forest, along the treeline, or at the edges of trails.

HOW TO HARVEST
Red berries ripen in August.

HOW TO USE
Just like its name, skunk currants taste skunky or beery. Use skunk currants as you would cultivated currants or, if you find enough, make beer or wine.

BERRIES

BERRIES

Skunk Current Pie

Chef Nick Giles, The Gathering Place, private catering

Pie crust
2 cups flour
1 cup cold butter
Pinch salt
1/3 cup buttermilk (cream or milk will also work)

Mix the flour and salt. Cut the butter into cubes. In a food processor or by hand work the butter into the flour until the butter chunks are pea sized and the mixture looks a bit shaggy and mealy. Add the buttermilk and work the dough only until it comes together. Do not over knead.

Wrap the dough in plastic wrap and refrigerate for at least 2 hours. Once the dough has been chilled, flour a work surface and roll the dough out until it's about half a centimetre thick and about 10 to 15 centimetres larger in diameter than the pie plate. Fit the dough to the plate, trim off the excess but leave a little overhang. Crimp the edges or leave as is for a rustic look. Refrigerate again for at least 1 hour.

Cut a piece of parchment paper to fit the bottom of the crust, leaving the edges exposed. Place the parchment in the crust and fill with dried beans, peas, or lentils. These "baking weights" will help prevent the crust from shrinking while the crust bakes, so that your pie will have a nice shape and cut evenly.

Bake the pie with the weights in a preheated 375°F oven for about 15 minutes or until the edges start to turn golden brown. Remove the parchment paper and weights and continue baking until the freshly exposed crust area is golden brown. Allow the crust to cool while you make the pastry cream.

BERRIES

Pastry cream
1 cup + 3 tbsp whole milk
3 egg yolks
1/3 cup cornstarch
2 gelatin sheets

½ vanilla bean split lengthwise
¼ cup white sugar
½ cup butter

Scald the milk with the vanilla bean in a pot. Whip the sugar, egg yolks, and corn starch until doubled in size and smooth. Soften the gelatin in cold water. Once the milk is hot, add slowly to the egg/sugar mix, whisking constantly, until fully incorporated. Transfer the milk mixture back to the pot and cook until mixture reaches 80°C. Remove from heat. Stir in the butter and gelatin sheets until dissolved. Strain the mixture to remove any lumps. Allow to cool slightly.

Pour the cooled cream into the prebaked pie crust. Place in the refridgeator for at least 4 hours to set. In the meantime, make the jelly.

Skunk currant jelly
1 lb currants
1 cup water
3 gelatin sheets

2 cups sugar
Pinch of salt

Combine the currants, sugar, and water in a pot. Cook at medium heat for 20 to 30 minutes, or until the mixture has reduced by about half and is thickening.

While the jam is reducing, soften the gelatin sheets in cold water. Remove the berry mixture from heat. Let sit 5 minutes, then dissolve softened gelatin sheets in the jam.

Allow the jelly to cool to room temperature. Spread the jelly evenly across the top of the already set pastry cream pie. Refrigerate the pie, ideally overnight but at least 4 to 6 hours. If everything goes as planned, you'll have a nice, clean, layered pie.

BERRIES

BERRIES

SQUASHBERRY

Moose berry
Viburnum edule

July - August

WHAT IS IT?
Squashberry, an upright deciduous shrub to 2 metres tall, looks like a cross between an alder (for leaf texture and shrub height) and a currant bush (for leaf shape). Its opposite toothed leaves are 4 to 8 centimetres long with three hairless lobes and turn purple in autumn. Clusters of tiny, white, five-petalled flowers, often paired, bloom in June. The bright red fruit have a large flattened seed.

Squashberry is more common in Newfoundland than high-bush cranberry, its close relative, and its fruit tend to be sweeter.

HOW TO HARVEST
Harvest ripe fruit in September.

HOW TO USE
Make jam, jelly, or wine; remove the flattened seeds before eating.

BERRIES

BERRIES

WILD HASKAP

Mountain fly honeysuckle, northern fly honeysuckle *Lonicera villiosa*

July - August

WHAT IS IT?
Wild haskap is non-climbing member of the honeysuckle family. It is a short, upright shrub, usually less than 1 metre tall, found in wetlands and on banks and barrens. Its paired oblong untoothed leaves are dark green with a light green lower surface; both surfaces are covered in fine hairs. Its bell-shaped yellow flowers grow in pairs.

Its blue to purple fruit appear to have two eyes—a key distinguishing feature. The fruit are irregular oblong-shaped and ripen in midsummer.

Haskap fruit are delicious, packed with nutrients, and uncommon—so enjoy them when you find some.

HOW TO HARVEST
Fruit grow under the leaves and are often hidden. Gently push aside the branches and look for clusters of slightly soft purple fruit.

HOW TO USE
Snack on haskap fruit as you hike. If you find enough, make jam, jelly, or add to baked goods.

BERRIES

WILD STRAWBERRY

Woodland strawberry
Fragaria virginiana, Fragaria vesca

July - August

WHAT IS IT?

Wild strawberries are tiny red strawberries found in clearings and fields and along the edges of forests. Although only 1 to 2 centimetres in diameter, the fruit pack a flavour punch way beyond that of large cultivated strawberries.

Wild strawberry plants are small (10 to 20 centimetres tall) and spread by runners. Its leaves have three toothed lobes. The five-petalled white flowers have a distinct yellow centre, followed by red fruit.

HOW TO HARVEST

Pick strawberries as they ripen in mid- to late July through early August. Harvest leaves any time while they are still green.

HOW TO USE

Wild strawberries are candy-sweet. Eat raw or make ice cream, cake, or other baked goods. Try wild strawberry and rhubarb jam.

Make tea with fresh or dried strawberry leaves.

BERRIES

BERRIES

Wild Strawberry Jam-Jams
Graham and Kelly Parisien, Nourish Bakery, Paradise

Jam (makes about 2 cups)
1½ cups wild strawberries
2 tbsp water
¾ cup cane sugar
¼ tsp pectin powder

Remove the stems from the wild strawberries and add the berries to a small saucepan with 2 tbsp water. Bring to a simmer, reduce the heat, and cook on low for 5 minutes.

Mix the pectin powder with the sugar, then add to the simmering strawberries. Stir to incorporate and let simmer another 5 minutes, until thickened.

Pour into a heat-safe bowl and let set in the refrigerator for an hour, or until cool.

Pipe or spoon onto cookies.

Cookies (for about 38 sandwiches)
¾ cup brown sugar
¾ cup butter
1 egg
½ cup molasses
2 cups gluten-free flour (we use an all-purpose/rice blend)
3 tsp salt
1 tsp baking powder
Xanthan gum

Beat the butter and sugar until light and fluffy.

Add the egg and molasses and mix until fully incorporated.

Combine the dry ingredients and add to the wet. Beat until combined, stopping to scrape the bowl if needed.

Wrap in plastic wrap and refrigerate at least 2 hours, or until firm.

BERRIES

Roll out on a lightly floured surface to ¼-centimetre thickness. Using a 5-centimetre round cookie cutter, cut the cookies and bake at 350°F for 10 minutes.
Once cool, fill with jam.

FLOWER POWER

Add a pop of colour to your plate with common wildflowers! This section introduces several beautiful, edible blooms that make wonderful garnishes, salad toppings, and infusions.

Candy wildflower leaves and petals to decorate cakes and baked goods. Daisy and marsh violet leaves (as well as the blooms) are delightful additions to salads. Make jelly from Queen Anne's lace. Make daisy capers by pickling unopened buds in a salt brine.

Of course, these aren't the only edible flowers you'll find in the wild. Others are featured elsewhere in this book, including fireweed, rose, forsythia, and elderflower. It is important not to assume that all beautiful blooms are edible. Some are toxic, even deadly.

FLOWER POWER

Blue violet.

Forget-me-not.

Marsh marigold.

Coltsfoot.

FLOWER POWER

BLUE VIOLET
(*Viola* spp.) grows close to the ocean in grassy areas. The plants reach 15 centimetres tall and have heart-shaped leaves. Blooms are blue to purple, less commonly white or yellow; all are edible. Add tender leaves to salads.

COLTSFOOT
(*Tussilago farfara*) flowers emerge before its leaves, making this one of the first wildflowers to appear in the spring. Each flower stem ends in a single bright yellow 1.5-centimetre-wide bloom. Stem leaves are reduced to bracts; basal leaves are heart-shaped. Toss flowers in salads or dry and add to baked goods or fritters.

FORGET-ME-NOT
(*Myosotis laxa*), found in grassy areas, gardens, lawns, and wet areas. These plants grow in mats, with spindly stems and small five-petalled blue to purple mild-tasting flowers. Use as a garnish.

MARSH MARIGOLD
(*Caltha palustris*), which thrives in wet or damp soil, are 20 to 40 centimetres tall with kidney-shaped leaves. The flower heads can be pickled, capered, or steamed. Harvest leaves and stems until the flowers disappear. Steam or boil leaves before eating. **Do not eat raw marsh marigold leaves; they contain small amounts of helleborin, a toxin that is removed by boiling**.

FLOWER POWER

Oxeye daisy.

Queen Anne's lace.

FLOWER POWER

OXEYE DAISY

(*Leucanthemum vulgare*) is an introduced species commonly found along roadsides and in fields and other disturbed areas. The flowers have yellow centres and up to 35 white rays. The leaves have a mild mustard-like flavour; add to salads or sandwiches. Flowers can be eaten raw or pickled; capered daisy buds are a favourite.

QUEEN ANNE'S LACE

(wild carrot, *Daucus carota*) is a biennial growing 30 to 90 centimetres tall in disturbed areas. Its leaves are carrot-like; the stems are covered in soft hairs. Lacy flat-topped flower clusters bloom from July to September. The long taproot can be eaten while the plants are young (first-year plants prior to flowering). Dry the seeds and use as a spice. Flower heads can be eaten raw, battered and fried, or used to make jelly. **Caution: do not confuse Queen Anne's lace with cow parsnip or types of hemlock, which should not be eaten.**

LICHEN IT

Lichens are not plants but result from a symbiotic partnership between a fungus and an alga (or cyanobacteria). Algae can conduct photosynthesis—fungi cannot—and produce energy from the sun to contribute to the organism's growth.

Thousands of species are found worldwide, in a variety of colours, shapes, and locations. In Newfoundland, lichens are common and widespread on rocks, trees, and other substrates. One species, commonly known as caribou moss, is collected for food.

LICHEN IT

CARIBOU MOSS

Reindeer moss, reindeer lichen
Cladonia rangiferina

Year round

WHAT IS IT?

Caribou moss is not moss but a lichen. Caribou moss grows slowly, a few millimetres a year, in dry, open areas such as berry heaths, coastal barrens, and along pole lines and other disturbed sites.

Caribou moss has a highly branched, bushy structure and is white to grey to pale yellow-green. It does not flower but it does develop bright red reproductive parts.

This lichen gets its common name from the caribou and moose that graze on it.

HOW TO HARVEST

Cut chunks of caribou moss from dry patches; never rip the holdfast from the soil. Harvest judiciously, being respectful of its slow growth.

HOW TO USE

Clean caribou moss thoroughly before eating. Make a salty, woodsy snack by tossing in oil, frying, and sprinkling with salt.

Caribou Moss Two Ways
Reindeer Lichen, Crispy and Candied

Nick King, Ollie's Pasta, St. John's

Crispy fried moss
Soak the moss overnight with enough water to cover. This process removes impurities and bitter natural acids. Drain and thoroughly remove any dirt, branches, and leaves from the harvest.

Blanch the moss in boiling water for about 5 minutes.

Strain and deep-fry quickly in canola or another neutral oil at 370 to 375°F, until crisp but not coloured. This will happen quickly and the oil will likely spit, so be careful as you add the moss and be quick to remove it.

Cool on a sheet pan lined with a wire rack or alternatively on paper towel to catch the excess oil.

Liberally season with salt or other seasoning of choice.

This provides a crisp garnish with mushroom-like earthiness to complement wild game, grilled meats, a salad, or even as a potato-chip-like snack.

Candied moss, a.k.a. forest candy
Make a simple syrup. This is just a ratio of sugar to water of 1:1 by weight. Bring the sugar and water to a simmer, dissolve sugar and slightly reduce to create a syrup consistency.

Submerge the cleaned moss in a pot of hot simple syrup (about 300°F on a candy thermometer) and transfer to a silpat or parchment-lined baking sheet.

Let cool, and bake at a low temperature of about 240°F, or until the moss begins to harden to a candy-like texture.

LICHEN IT

INDEX

By common name

alder 145
alsike clover 27
American green alder 145
apple 175
aronia berry 217

bakeapple 204
balsam fir 148
beach pea 91
beachgrass 111
birch 151
black currant 180
black elderberry 179
black spruce 163
black tang 129
blackberry 210
blackberry (crowberry) 225
bladderwrack 129
blue marsh violet 265
blueberry 213
bog corn 114
bog myrtle 168
broadleaf plantain 74
bittercress 56
bull rush 114
bunchberry 214

capillaire 224
caribou moss 271
cattails 114
chickweed 63
chokecherry 219
chokeberry 217
chuckley pear 221
cloudberry 204
clover 27
coltsfoot 265
common juniper 152
common nettle 51
corn lily 29
crabapple 175
crackerberry 214
crackerjacks 214
cranberry 222
creeping snowberry 224
crowberry 225
curly dock 79

currants 180

damson 182
dandelion 31
dewberry 228
dogberry 231
dogmint 124

Easter tree 187
eastern larch 171

fiddlehead 36
field pennycress 68
fireweed 38
forget-me-not 265
forsythia 187
fox berry 236

garden sorrel 79
goosefoot 64
goosetongue 93
goutweed 43
ground elder 43
ground juniper 152
ground raspberry 228

hairy plumboy 228
herb of St. Barbara 56
high-bush cranberry 233
Japanese knotweed 44
Juneberry 221
juniper (shrub) 152
juniper (tree) 171

Labrador tea 156
lamb's quarter 64
lilac 189
lingonberry 236

magna-tea berry 224
maidenhair berry 224
maple 158
marshberry 222
marsh marigold 265
moose berry 255
moss berry 225
mountain ash 231

mountain cranberry 236
mountain fly honeysuckle 257
mountain maple 158

northern fly honeysuckle 257
northern wild raisin 234
Norway maple 158

oarweed 131
orach 94
ostrich fern 36
oxeye daisy 267
oysterleaf 97

partridgeberry 236
pennycress 68
pin cherry 240
pineappleweed 71
plantain 74
plum 192

Queen Anne's lace 267

raspberry 243
red berry 236
red clover 27
red currant 180
red dulse 134
red maple 158
reindeer lichen 271
reindeer moss 271
rhubarb 194
river mint 118
rose 247
roseroot 98
rowanberry 231

sandwort 100
Saskatoon berry 221
Scotch lovage 105
sea bluebells 97
sea chickweed 100
sea lettuce 136
sea lungwort 97
sea rocket 108
sea sandwort 100
seaside plantain 93

serviceberry 221
shadblow 221
sheep sorrel 79
shepherd's purse 76
shining rose 247
shrub rose 247
skunk currant 250
snowberry 224
sorrel 79
speckled alder 145
spruce 163
squashberry 255
stinging nettle 51
stonecrop 84
strand wheat 111
sugar kelp 139
sweet gale 168
sycamore maple 158

tamarack 171
tea berries 224

Virginia rose 247

watercress 123
white clover 27
white currant 180
white spruce 163
wild basil 124
wild carrot 267
wild chamomile 71
wild haskap 257
wild hops 199
wild mustard 56
wild plantain 74
wild quinoa 64
wild spinach 64
wild strawberry 258
wintercress 56
woodland strawberry 258

yarrow 58

By Latin name

Abies balsamea 148
Acer platanoides 158
Acer pseudoplatanus 158
Acer rubrum 158
Achillea millefolium 58
Aegopodium podagraria 43
Alnus spp. 145
Amelanchier spp. 221
Ammophila breviligulata 111
Atriplex glabriuscula 94
Atriplex patula 94

Barbarea vulgaris 56
Betula spp. 151

Cakile edentula 108
Caltha palustris 265
Capsella bursa-pastoris 76
Chamaenerion angustifolium 38
Chenopodium album 64
Cladonia rangiferina 271
Clinopodium vulgare 124
Clintonia borealis 29
Cornus canadensis 214

Daucus carota 267

Empetrum nigrum 225

Fallopia japonica 44
Forsythia spp. 187
Fragaria virginiana 258
Fragaria vesca 258
Fucus vesiculosus 129

Gaultheria hispidula 224

Honckenya peploides 100
Humulus lupulus 199

Juniperus communis 152

Laminaria digitata 131
Laminaria saccharina 139
Larix laricina 171
Lathyrus japonicus 91
Leucanthemum vulgare 267
Leymus arenarius 111
Ligusticum scoticum 105
Lonicera villosa 257

Malus pumila 175
Matricaria discoidea 71
Matteuccia struthiopteris 36
Mentha arvensis 118
Mentha cardiaca 118
Mertensia maritima 97
Myosotis laxa 265
Myrica gale 168

Nasturtium microphyllum 123

Palmaria palmata 134
Photinia floribunda 217
Photinia melanocarpa 217
Picea glauca 163
Picea mariana 163

Plantago major 74
Plantago maritima 93
Prunus domestica 182
Prunus pensylvanica 240
Prunus sp. 192
Prunus virginiana 219

Rheum rhabarbarum 194
Rhodiola rosea 98
Rhododendron groenlandicum 156
Ribes glanulosum 250
Ribes spp. 180
Rosa spp. 247
Rubus canadensis 210
Rubus chamaemorus 204
Rubus idaeus 243
Rubus pubescens 228
Rumex acetosa 79
Rumex acetosella 79
Rumex crispus 79

Sambucus nigra 179
Sedum spp. 84
Sorbus spp. 231
Stellaria media 63
Syringa vulgaris 189

Taraxacum officinale 31
Thlaspi arvense 68
Trifolium hybridum 27
Trifolium pretense 27
Trifolium repens 27
Tussilago farfara 265
Typha latifolia 114

Ulva lactuca 136
Urtica dioica 51

Vaccinium angustifolium 213
Vaccinium macrocarpon 222
Vaccinium oxycoccus 222
Vaccinium vitis-idaea 236
Viburnum edule 255
Viburnum nudum var. cassinoides 234
Viburnum opulus 233
Viola spp. 265

PHOTO CREDITS

Shawn Dawson: all sketches, 41 (bottom right), 52, 53, 57 (bottom), 70, 77 (bottom left), 88, 90, 92, 96, 98, 101, 104, 106, 107, 109, 115 (right), 119 (top), 122, 125, 133, 150, 153 (bottom), 157 (bottom), 160, 161, 172, 174 (top), 176, 178, 183, 184, 186, 188, 193, 195 (top), 200 (top), 202, 211 (bottom), 212 (top left), 215 (bottom), 223 (bottom left), 225, 229, 230 (top left, bottom right), 222 (top right), 242 (top), 246, 249, 258 (bottom), 264 (top right, bottom right), 268.

Robert Flogaus-Faust: 254 (top, licensed by CC-BY-4.0).

GeoO: 69 (bottom right, licensed by CC-BY-SA 4.0).

Roger Griffith: 232 (bottom left, licensed by CC-BY-SA 4.0).

Berger Harald: 220 (top left, licensed by CC-BY-2.5).

Adam Lannon: 35, 55.

Matt Lavin: 69 (bottom left, licensed by CC-BY-SA 2.0).

Stephanie Mackenzie: 191.

Mako: 181 (bottom left, licensed by CC-BY-SA 2.0).

Maria Martin: 41 (top, bottom left).

James H. Miller and Ted Bodner: 235 (top, licensed by CC-BY-3.0).

Colin Moïse: 155.

Ritche Perez: cover, 4, 9, 12, 14, 18, 19, 21, 22, 23, 24, 26 (bottom), 30, 32, 33, 39, 42, 45, 46, 47, 48, 49, 50, 57 (top), 59, 60, 62, 65, 67, 71, 75, 78, 80, 81, 82, 85, 102, 112, 116, 119 (bottom), 121, 126, 128, 129, 130, 131, 134, 135, 136, 137, 138, 139, 141, 142, 144, 146, 147, 149, 153 (top), 157 (top), 159 (top), 162, 164, 165, 167, 169, 170, 174 (bottom left), 181 (top left), 197, 198, 200 (bottom), 201 (bottom), 207, 209, 211 (top), 212 (bottom), 215 (top), 216 (top), 218 (bottom), 220 (top right, bottom), 223 (top, bottom right), 239, 241 (top), 242 (bottom), 244, 251 (top), 256 (top, bottom right), 256 (bottom left), 258 (top), 262, 266 (bottom), 274, 275, 280.

Stephanie Porter: 26 (top), 28, 77 (top, bottom right), 95, 110, 115 (left), 150, 159 (bottom), 174 (bottom right), 195 (bottom), 205 (bottom), 212 (top right), 220 (top left), 227, 230 (top right, bottom left), 235 (bottom), 237, 241 (bottom), 270, 273.

Dave Powell, USDA Forest Service: 254 (bottom left).

Steve Redman, National Park Service: 264 (top right).

Arnstein Ronning: 205 (top, licensed by CC-BY-3.0).

Miika Silfverberg: 37 (bottom right, licensed by CC-BY-SA 2.0).

Ryan Somma: 37 (top, licensed by CC-BY-SA 2.0).

James St. John: 11 (licensed by CC-BY-2.0).

Matthew Swift: 87.

Tirapolsky: 181 (top right, licensed by CC-BY-SA 4.0).

Zimmerzute: 37 (bottom left, licensed by CC-BY-2.5)

ACKNOWLEDGEMENTS

First and foremost, thank you to all of the local talented chefs who inspire me every day with their passion for cooking with the food that comes from our extraordinary, rugged island. I have made so many amazing friends through the back doors of our restaurants—thank you for the support and encouragement and for feeding me during deliveries.

Sincere thanks as well to all of the home cooks who have shown so much interest at the St. John's Farmers' Market over the years. Just as the professional chefs have, you have pushed me to discover more about Newfoundland's wild edibles.

Thank you to everyone who contributed a recipe to this book. I am grateful to work with such a wonderful community.

Thanks to Jon Howse and Sylvie Mitford of The Boreal Diner in Bonavista for hosting the first Forager's Dinner. That event was the spark that started this book.

To my dearest Celeste Mah, thank you for writing such a heartfelt foreword and always feeding me the delicious treats you make with wild food.

To my friends and family for always being so supportive, thank you. A big shout-out to the SMM (Single Mushroom Men)!

Ritche Perez, you are a true talent, my friend. Thank you for all of the great photos.

And to my dear friend and editor, Stephanie Porter. I would never have finished this book without you. Thank you for your patience, constant reminders about my homework, and your help pulling this all together. Thank you to Gavin Will and everyone at Boulder Books.

To my good friend Elke Dettmer, thank you for inviting me to your homestead. It has been an inspirational place to write this book. Finally, and most of all, I would like to pay homage to the beautiful and bountiful island I am fortunate to call home.

Top, from left: Shawn Dawson, Celeste Mah (pasty chef, Raymonds), Mark Wilson (NL Organics Ltd., Newfoundland Gourmet Mushrooms), Scott Fowlow (Barking Kettle), and Ross Larkin (chef de cuisine, Raymonds) enjoying fine-dining wild food at Raymonds Restaurant, St. John's. Below: Dawson and Wilson with chef Nick Van Mele at the St. John's Farmers' Market.

ABOUT THE AUTHOR

Shawn Dawson (a.k.a. Flossman Dandy Cabbage) grew up on Newfoundland's Southern Shore, close to the land and sea. His childhood was spent fishing cod with his dad, picking wild greens with his nan, rabbit hunting with his uncles, and spending most of his days outside in awe of the wonder of it all. Shawn has been foraging plants and mushrooms for St. John's finest restaurants for years under the business name Barking Kettle. His table at the St. John's Farmers' Market is a must-visit for seasonal and preserved wild food, as well as stories and tips. Shawn offers popular foraging tours, and frequently collaborates with local chefs for dinners, events, and food festivals. Shawn has extensive knowledge of local foraging and a true love for exploring Newfoundland and Labrador.